The best Year 2 Maths practice from CGP!

This brilliant CGP Targeted Question Book is perfect for
helping pupils to build their Year 2 Maths skills.

It's crammed full of questions covering everything on the Year 2 Programme of Study,
as well as Warm Up Questions to help get pupils thinking.

Not only that, we've also included Objectives Tests at the start and end of the book,
and regular Progress Tests throughout — perfect for seeing how pupils are doing.
There are even answers to every question at the back. You're welcome!

What CGP is all about

Our sole aim here at CGP is to produce the highest quality
books — carefully written, immaculately presented and
dangerously close to being funny.

Then we work our socks off to get them out to you
— at the cheapest possible prices.

Contents

About This Book 1

Year One Objectives Test 2

Section One — Number and Place Value

Place Value 6
Numbers to 100 7
Twos, Threes, Fives and Tens 8
The Number Line 9
Partitioning 10
Ordering and Comparing Numbers 11
Solving Number Problems 12

Progress Test 1 14

Section Two — Addition and Subtraction

Number Bonds 16
Adding 17
Subtracting 19
Checking 21

Section Three — Multiplication and Division

Times Tables 22
Using Times Tables Facts 24
Multiplying 25
Dividing 26
Double and Half 27

Section Four — Fractions

Thirds and Quarters 28
Fractions of Amounts 29
Equivalent Fractions 31

Progress Test 2 32

Section Five — Measurement

Units 34
Measuring 35
Comparing Measurements 36
Money 37
Sums with Money 38
Time 39
Comparing Time 40

Section Six — Geometry

Flat (2D) Shapes 41
Solid (3D) Shapes 42
Sorting Shapes 43
Drawing Shapes and Patterns 44
Position 46
Direction and Turns 47

Progress Test 3 48

Section Seven — Statistics

Tables 52
Tally Charts 53
Block Diagrams 54
Pictograms 55

Year Two Objectives Test 56

Answers 60

Published by CGP

Editors:
Martha Bozic, Sammy El-Bahrawy, Sarah George, Hannah Lawson,
Sean McParland, Alison Palin, Caley Simpson.

ISBN: 978 1 78908917 2

With thanks to Glenn Rogers and Gareth Mitchell for the proofreading.
With thanks to Jan Greenway for the copyright research.

Images on the cover and throughout the book © Educlips
Clipart from Corel®

Printed by W&G Baird Ltd, Antrim.
Based on the classic CGP style created by Richard Parsons.

Text, design, layout and original illustrations © Coordination Group Publications Ltd. (CGP) 2022
All rights reserved.

Photocopying this book is not permitted, even if you have a CLA licence.
Extra copies are available from CGP with next day delivery • 0800 1712 712 • www.cgpbooks.co.uk

About This Book

This Book is Full of Year 2 Maths Questions

This book has questions on all the maths for Year 2. It matches our Year 2 Study Book — this can help you if you get stuck.

This book covers the Attainment Targets for Year 2 of the National Curriculum.

Some pages have Warm Up Questions at the top in boxes like this. These will get you started on the topic. They're great to do out loud or in a group.

> **Warm Up Question**
> Starting at 6, count up in 2s. Stop when you get to 16.

The answers to all of the questions are at the back of the book.

There are Two Sorts of Tests in This Book

There are two Objectives Tests. The one at the front of the book tests that you remember the maths you learnt in Year 1. The one at the back is to see what you've learnt in Year 2.

There are three Progress Tests. Each one tests you on all the maths that has come before it. They help you see how you're doing with the topics covered so far.

There are Learning Objectives for Each Topic

Learning objectives say what you should be able to do.

A printable checklist of all the objectives can be found at cgpbooks.co.uk/PrimaryMathsLO or by scanning this QR code.

Use the tick boxes to show how happy you feel.

Tick here if you need a bit more practice.
Tick here if you're really struggling.
Tick here if you can do all the maths on the page.

"I can count in steps of 2, 3, 5 and 10."

Year One Objectives Test

1 Circle the plate that has the **most** sandwiches.

1 mark

2 Look at the pen and pencil below.

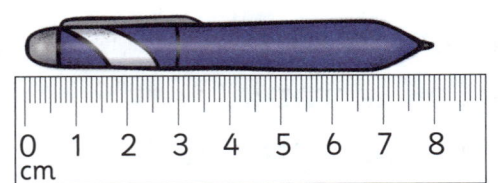 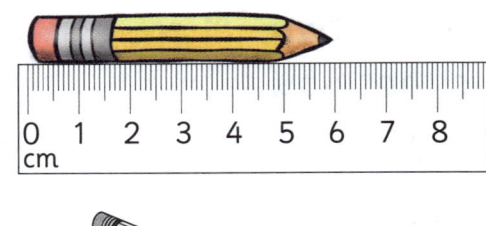

How long is the pen? ☐ cm

1 mark

Circle the word that makes this sentence **correct**.

The pencil is 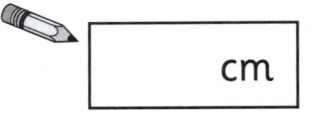 longer / shorter than the pen.

1 mark

3 Fill in the missing number in this list.

19   18   ☐   16   15   14

1 mark

Year One Objectives Test

4 Circle all of the shapes below that are **cubes**.

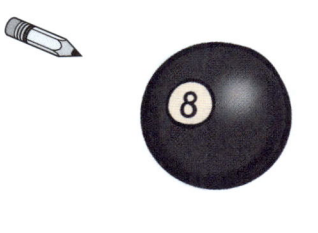

1 mark

5 Fill in the missing numbers in these sentences.

There are ☐ days in a week.

There are ☐ days in August.

1 mark

6 Use number bonds to answer these questions.

Circle the **two** numbers that **add together** to make 10.

1   8   5   7   2   4

1 mark

Fill in the missing number in this addition.

3 + ☐ = 20

1 mark

Year One Objectives Test

7 Draw the **next shape** in this pattern.

1 mark

8 Use the number line to fill in the boxes below.

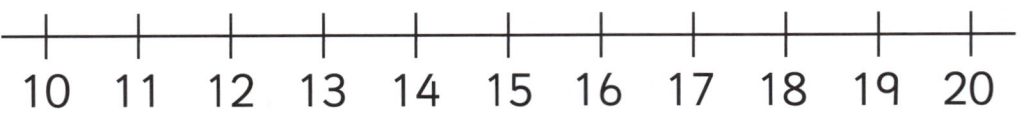

19 − 3 = ☐

The difference between 11 and 17 is ☐.

2 marks

9 Match the fractions to the amount that is shaded by drawing a line between them.

One half   One quarter

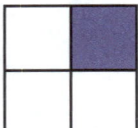   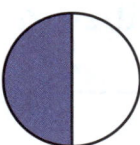   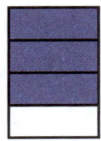

1 mark

Year One Objectives Test

10 Eggs come in **boxes of 6**. Hal has **two boxes**. How many eggs does he have in total?

  2 × 6 = ☐

1 mark

11 This arrow makes a **three-quarter** turn **anticlockwise**. Tick the box that shows the direction it is pointing now.

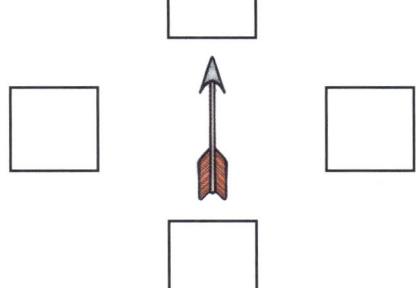

1 mark

12 Share these flowers into **four equal groups**. Then fill in the missing numbers below.

☐ ÷ 4 = ☐

1 mark

Score: ☐/15

Section One — Number and Place Value

Place Value

1) Write the missing numbers in the boxes.

43 has ☐ tens and ☐ ones.

89 has ☐ tens and ☐ ones.

2) Each picture shows a 2-digit number. Fill in the number of tens and ones, then write the number. The first one has been done for you.

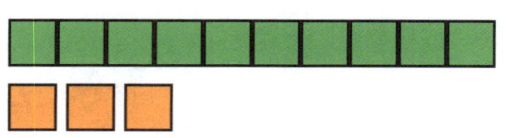 | 1 | Ten
                        | 3 | Ones   13

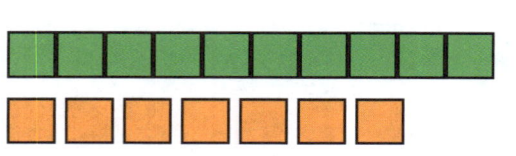   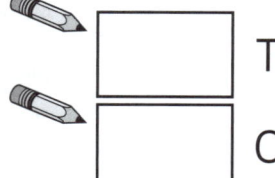   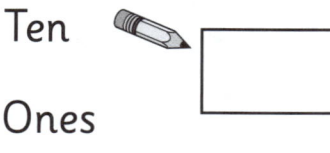

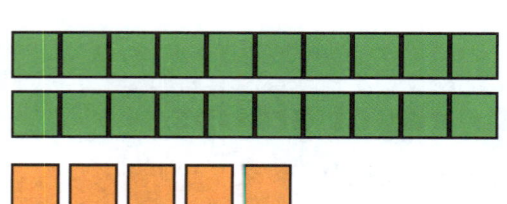      

3) Use **two** of these digits to make the **biggest** 2-digit number you can.

"I can recognise the place value of each digit in a two-digit number."

Numbers to 100

Warm Up Question

Read these numbers out loud.   17   54   90

1) Draw lines to match the words to the numbers.

Fourteen   Forty-one   Twenty-four

2) Write these words as **numbers**.

Eleven ⬜   Fifty-five ⬜

Thirty-nine ⬜   One hundred and ten ⬜

3) Write these numbers in **words**.

22 ⬜

98 ⬜

"I can read and write numbers up to at least 100 in numerals and words."

Section One — Number and Place Value

Twos, Threes, Fives and Tens

1 Fill in the missing numbers.

2 Count **forwards** in **tens** from the circled number. Circle each number you land on.

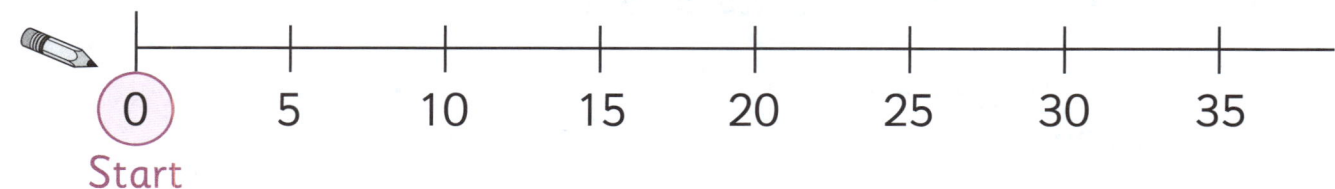

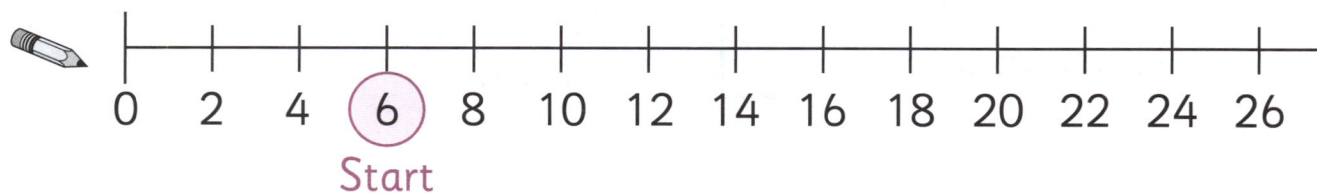

3 Fill in the next number in each list.

3   6   9   ☐

53   43   33   ☐

"I can count in steps of 2, 3, 5 and 10."

The Number Line

1) Fill in the gaps on the number line.

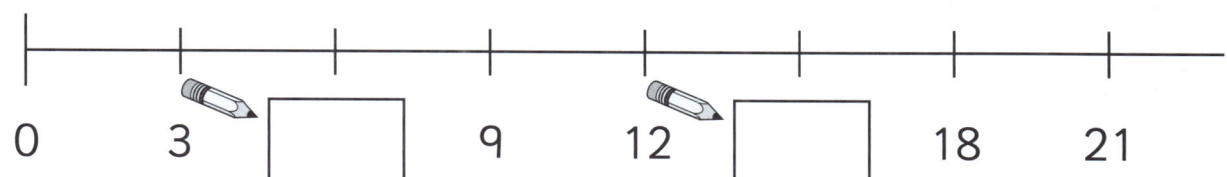

2) Find 35 on this number line.
Draw an arrow to show where it is.

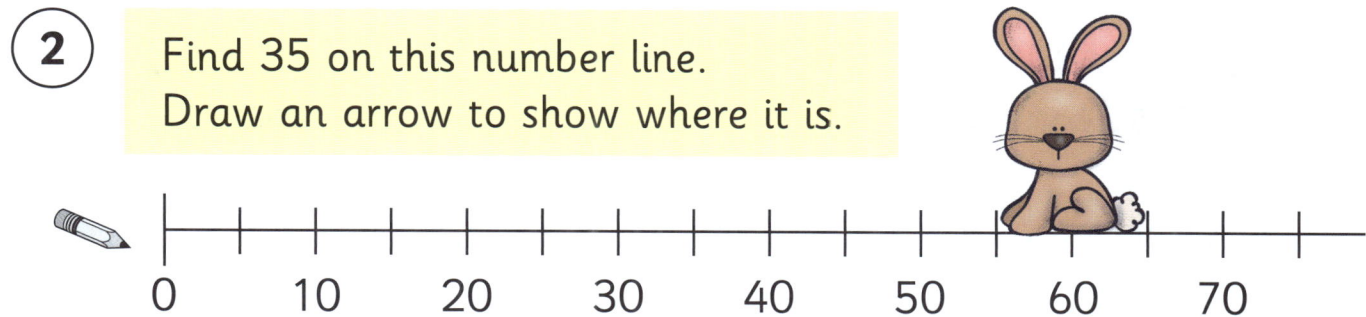

3) **Estimate** the numbers that the carrots are pointing to.

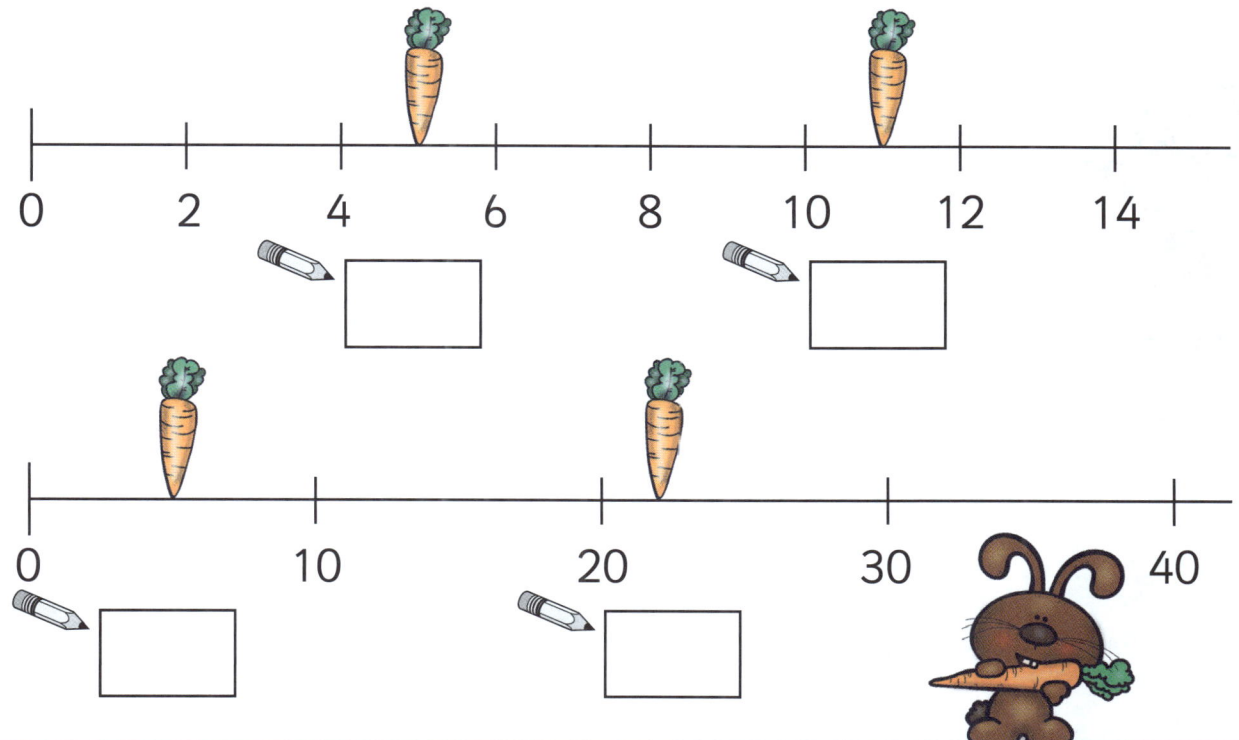

"I can find and estimate numbers on a number line."

Partitioning

> **Warm Up Questions**
>
> 1) Which of these numbers has 3 ones?   34   30   63
> 2) Which of these numbers has 8 tens?   81   18   8

1) Partition these numbers into **tens** and **ones**.

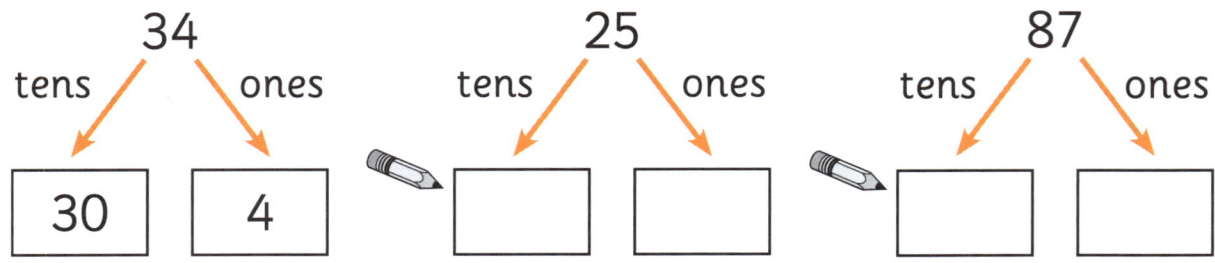

2) Put a **tick** in the box next to the correct sums. Put a **cross** next to the incorrect ones.

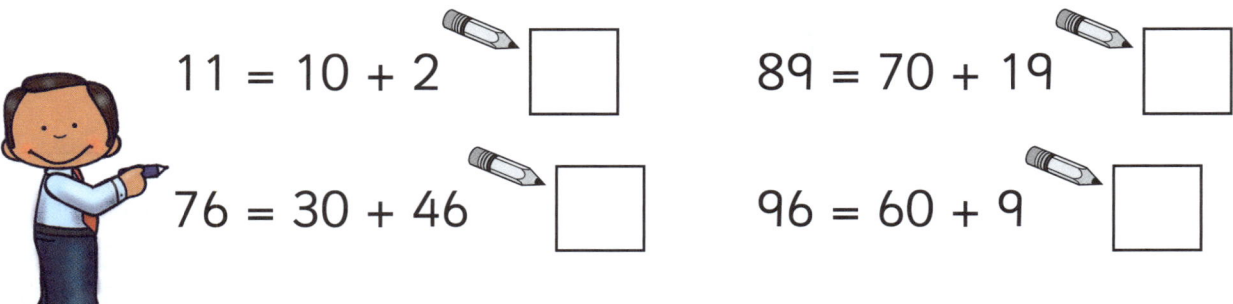

3) Partition the number 45 in **two** different ways.

45 = ☐ + ☐

45 = ☐ + ☐

"I can use partitioning to show numbers in different ways."

Ordering and Comparing Numbers

1) Circle the **biggest** number in each list.

    6   22   12   24

    55   50   54   45

2) Order the numbers on the stars from **smallest** to **biggest**.

26   47   27   43

☐   ☐   ☐   ☐

3) Draw enough flowers to make this correct.

🌸🌸🌸   <

4) Put **<, >** or **=** in each box to make these correct.

77 ☐ 23   3 + 2 ☐ 5   37 ☐ 79

"I can compare and order numbers from 0 to 100."

Section One — Number and Place Value

Solving Number Problems

① Noah has 5 pet fish and 3 pet mice. How many pets does he have in total? You can use the number line to help you.

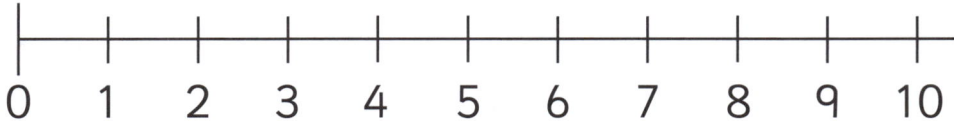

② There are 6 cats on a wall. 2 jump off. How many cats are left on the wall?

 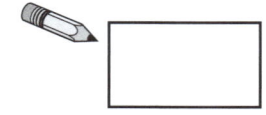

③ There are 10 birds in Sadie's garden. 7 more fly in. How many birds are there now?

Solving Number Problems

4 Muhammad has 30 oranges to sell. He sells 4. How many oranges does he have left to sell?

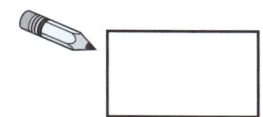

5 Gwen delivers 22 letters in the morning and 10 in the afternoon. How many letters does she deliver in total?

6 There are 48 books in a library. 20 books are taken out. How many books are left?

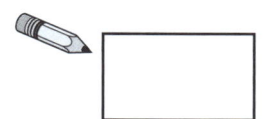

"I can solve problems using the things I've learned about numbers."

Progress Test 1

1 Look at the digit cards below.

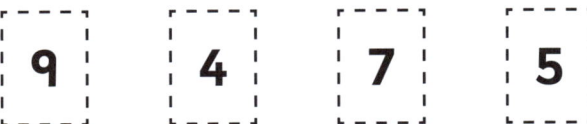

Use two of the cards to make:

the **biggest** 2-digit number you can.

the **smallest** 2-digit number you can.

2 marks

2 Write these numbers in **words**.

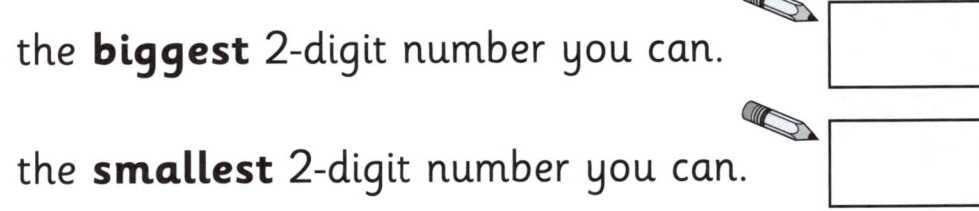

31

75

108

3 marks

3 Look at this number line.

Write the correct number in each box.

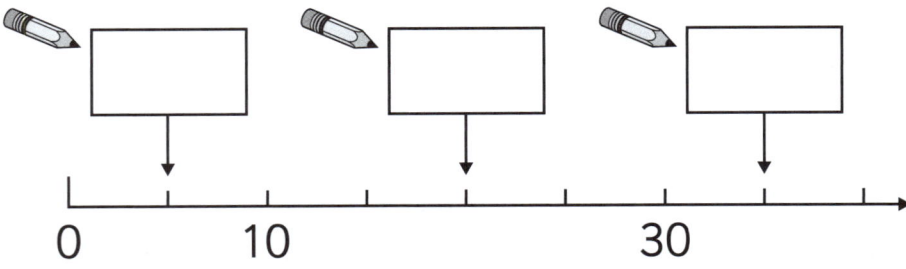

2 marks

Progress Test 1

Progress Test 1

4 Partition 94 in **two** different ways.

94 = ☐ + ☐

94 = ☐ + ☐ + ☐

2 marks

5 Fatima has a bag of 43 grapes. She eats 10 grapes. How many grapes are left?

☐

1 mark

6 Put **<**, **>** or **=** in the boxes to make these correct.

42 ☐ 68   3 + 7 ☐ 11 − 2

2 marks

7 Paul makes 50 cupcakes for a bake sale. Iris makes 29. How many cupcakes do they make altogether?

☐

1 mark

Score: ☐/13

Number Bonds

1 Join the pairs of numbers that add up to **20**.
One has been done for you.

19 —————————————— 7
                    \
14   15
                      \
 8   1

 5   12

13   6

2 Look at the addition below.
Fill in the boxes to make a matching **subtraction**.

12 + 5 = 17   ☐ − ☐ = ☐

3 Fill in the boxes to make pairs of numbers that add to **100**.

☐ 20   40 ☐   ☐ 70
(100)   (100)   (100)

"I know the number bonds up to 20 and can use number facts to answer questions."

Adding

Warm Up Question

Adam says that adding ones to a number can't change the digit in the tens place. Explain why he is wrong.

① Circle the correct word in each of these sums.

37 + 2 | ones / tens | = 57

62 + 3 | ones / tens | = 65

② Kian used partitioning to work out 21 + 56.
Fill in the gaps in his working below to make it correct.

21 = 20 + 1   56 = 50 + 6

20 + 50 = ☐   1 + 6 = ☐

☐ + ☐ = ☐

③ Work out these sums. Use the number line to help you.

40 45 50 55 60 65 70 75 80

48 + 23 = ☐   59 + 19 = ☐

Adding

④ Use **partitioning** to work out these sums.

41 + 30

25 + 32

76 + 14

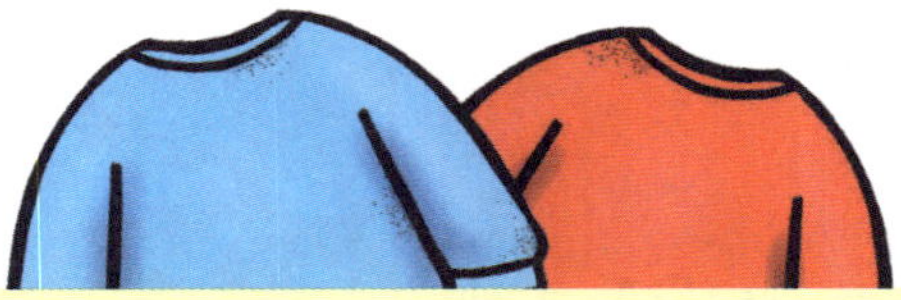

⑤ A shop sells 43 blue jumpers and 24 red jumpers. How many jumpers do they sell in total?

⑥ There are 52 sheep on a farm. 39 more sheep are born. How many sheep are there now?

"I can add using different methods, and can solve addition problems."

Section Two — Addition and Subtraction

Subtracting

1) Match each subtraction below to its answer. One has been done for you.

29 – 7   85 – 30   78 – 5   95 – 20   76 – 2

75   22   55   74   73

2) Use **partitioning** to work out these subtractions.

49 – 18

58 – 42

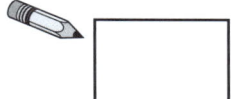

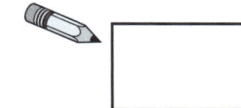

3) Fill in the missing number in this sentence. Use the number line to help you.

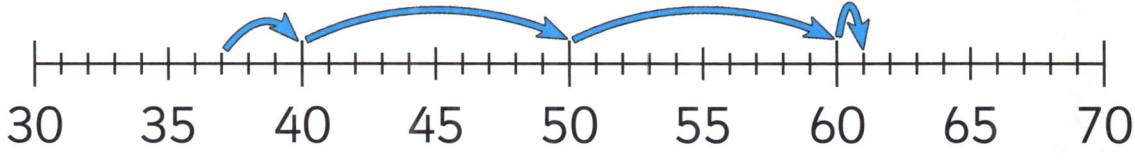

The difference between 37 and 61 is ☐.

Section Two — Addition and Subtraction

Subtracting

4 Work out these subtractions.
Use the number line to help you.

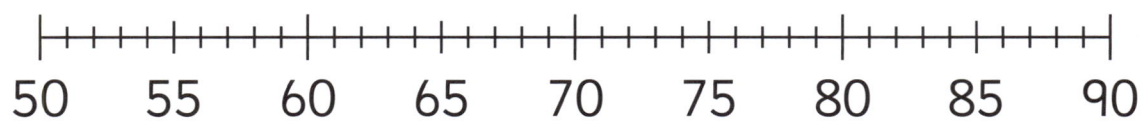

72 − 53 = ☐   83 − 67 = ☐

5 Maisie has 68 seeds. She gives 13 seeds to her friend.
How many seeds does Maisie have now?

6 Jack hit a cricket ball 36 times. Sue hit the ball 24 times.
How many more times did Jack hit the ball than Sue?

"I can subtract using different methods, and can solve subtraction problems."

Section Two — Addition and Subtraction

Checking

1) Circle the **inverse calculation** you could use to check each answer.

47 − 22 = 25   25 − 22   47 + 25   25 + 22

39 + 43 = 82   43 − 39   82 − 43   82 + 43

2) Tick the box next to each calculation below that is **true**.

34 + 19 − 19 = 19 ☐

52 − 25 + 25 = 52 ☐

66 + 31 − 31 = 66 ☐

3) Khelsea works out that 6 + 1 + 8 = 15. Write two different calculations she could use to check her answer.

☐ + ☐ + ☐ = ☐

☐ − ☐ − ☐ = ☐

"I know adding and subtracting are inverses and can use this to check my answers."

Section Two — Addition and Subtraction

Section Three — Multiplication and Division

Times Tables

Warm Up Questions

1) Starting at 6, count up in 2s.
   Stop when you get to 16.

2) Count up in 5s to find the missing numbers.

   10   ☐   ☐   25   ☐

1 Circle all the numbers that are in the 10 times table.

20   50   15   32

60   25   27   40   14

2 Fill in the numbers to complete these times tables facts.

7 × 2 = ☐   11 × 2 = ☐

6 × 5 = ☐   12 × 5 = ☐

8 × 10 = ☐   9 × 10 = ☐

Times Tables

3) Write down an even number that is **bigger** than 30 but **smaller** than 35.

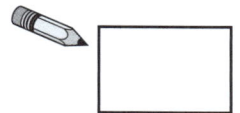

4) Circle the numbers that are odd **and** in the 5 times table.

5) Decide whether the numbers below are **odd** or **even**. Then circle the times tables they are in.
One has been done for you.

Number	Odd or Even?	Times Table
8	Even	② 5 10
45		2 5 10
24		2 5 10
20		2 5 10

"I know the 2, 5 and 10 times tables.
I know if numbers are odd or even."

Section Three — Multiplication and Division

Using Times Tables Facts

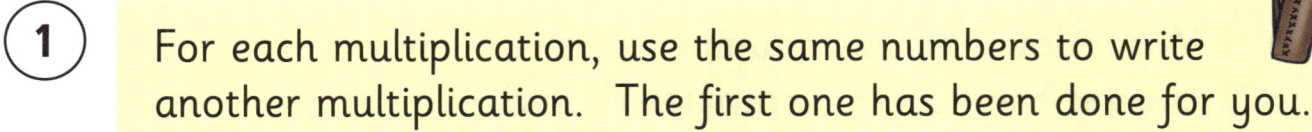

1 For each multiplication, use the same numbers to write another multiplication. The first one has been done for you.

7 × 5 = 35 ⟶ 5 × 7 = 35

9 × 10 = 90 ⟶ ☐ × ☐ = ☐

11 × 2 = 22 ⟶ ☐ × ☐ = ☐

2 Circle the **two** calculations that have the same answer.

10 × 8   6 × 10   6 × 5

2 × 8   8 × 10

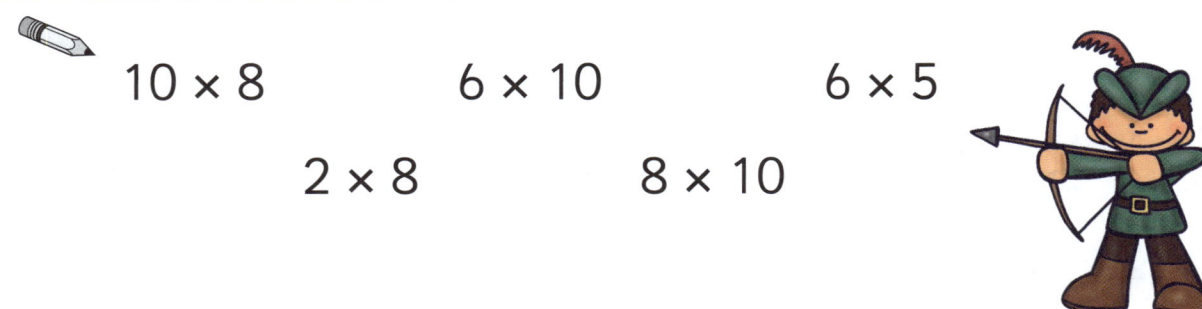

3 Use the times table facts to complete the matching divisions. The first one has been done for you.

9 × 2 = 18   18 ÷ 2 = 9   18 ÷ 9 = 2

7 × 5 = 35   35 ÷ 5 = ☐   35 ÷ 7 = ☐

5 × 10 = 50   50 ÷ 10 = ☐   50 ÷ 5 = ☐

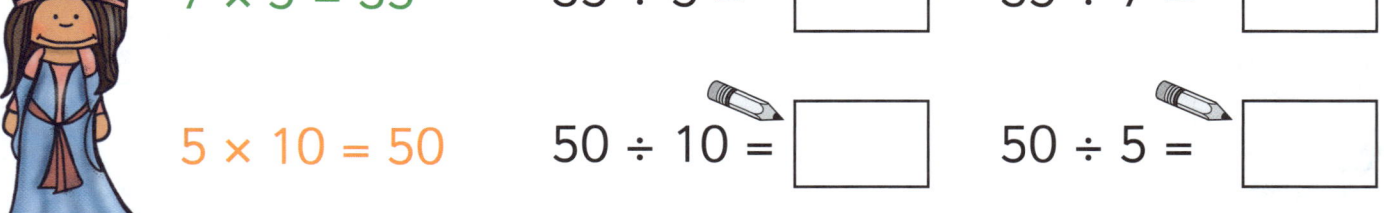

"I know that you can multiply in any order. I know dividing is the opposite of multiplying."

Section Three — Multiplication and Division

Multiplying

1) Fill in the missing numbers to find the total number of cherries.

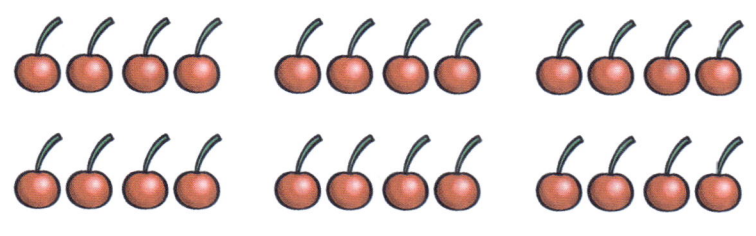

3 × ☐ = ☐

2) Use this number line to help you work out 3 × 4.

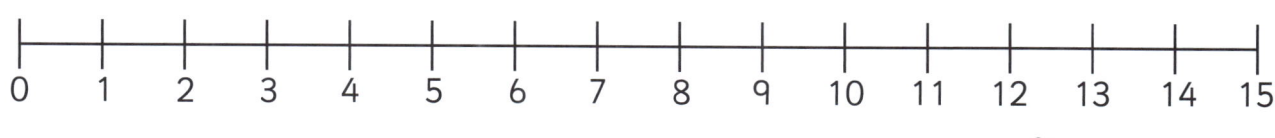

3 × 4 = ☐

3) Write a **repeated addition** calculation that gives the same answer as the multiplication. Then work out the answer. One has been done for you.

Multiplication	Repeated Addition	Answer
2 × 3	3 + 3	6
5 × 3		
3 × 3		
4 × 3		

"I can multiply by grouping pictures and by using mental maths."

Dividing

1 Divide the 18 crayons below into 3 equal groups to work out 18 ÷ 3.

18 ÷ 3 = ☐

2 Use this number line to help you work out 12 ÷ 2.

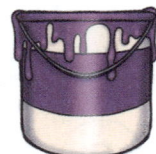

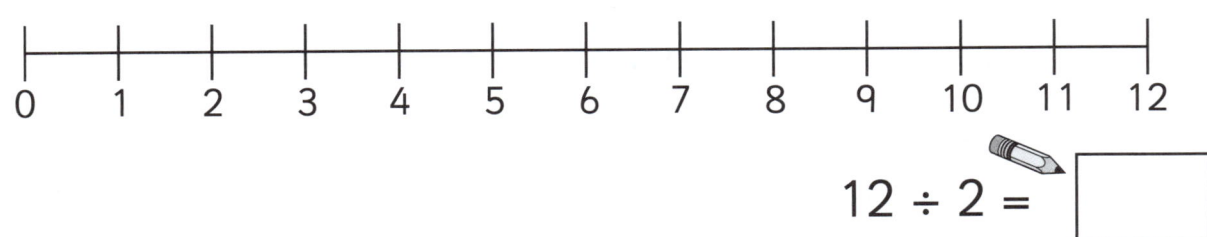

12 ÷ 2 = ☐

3 Farah has 25 paintbrushes. She divides them equally into 5 pots. How many paintbrushes are in each pot?

☐

"I can divide by grouping pictures and by using mental maths."

Section Three — Multiplication and Division

Double and Half

1 Match the number on the top row to the number that is **double** it on the bottom row. One has been done for you.

10   5   12   4

10   8   24   20

2 Complete the sentences below.

Half of 16 is ☐ .   Double 12 is ☐ .

3 A wizard has 9 toads. He uses a magic spell to **double** the number of toads. How many toads does he have now?

4 Fill in the gaps in the calculations below.

$\frac{1}{2}$ of 14 = ☐ $\frac{1}{2}$ of 22 = ☐

"I can find double and half by multiplying and dividing by 2."

Section Three — Multiplication and Division

Thirds and Quarters

1 Circle the shapes below that have $\frac{1}{4}$ shaded.

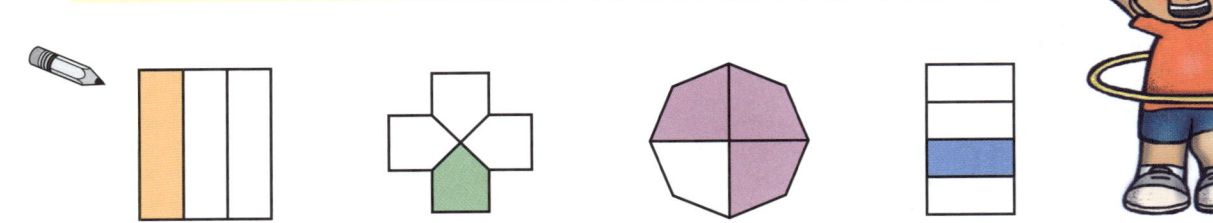

2 Colour in the fraction given for each shape.

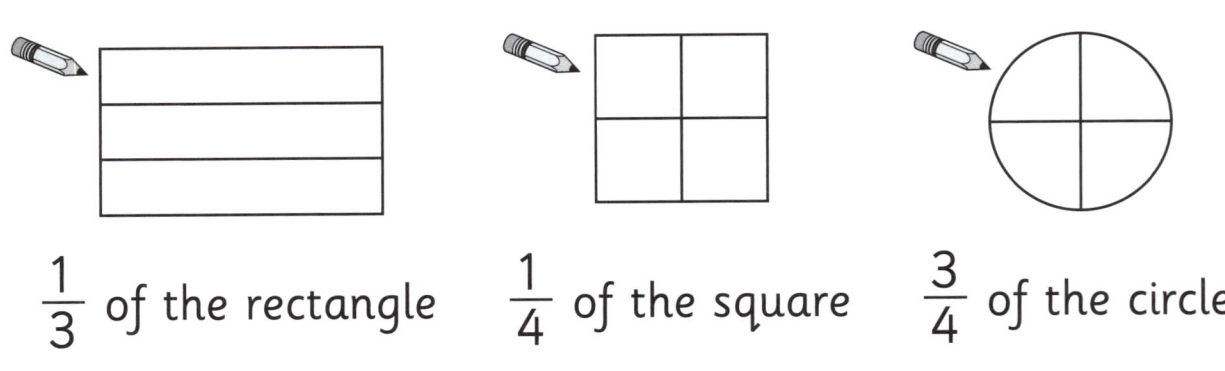

$\frac{1}{3}$ of the rectangle $\frac{1}{4}$ of the square $\frac{3}{4}$ of the circle

3 Look at these shapes. Circle **true** or **false** for each sentence below. The first one has been done for you.

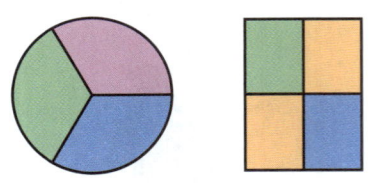

One quarter of the rectangle is blue.    (true) / false

One third of the circle is green.    true / false

Three quarters of the rectangle is orange.    true / false

"I can recognise and name fractions such as one third, one quarter and three quarters."

Fractions of Amounts

1 Here is a set of 4 beetles. Colour **half** of the set blue.

2 Look at these frogs.

What fraction of the frogs are **orange**?

What fraction of the frogs are **blue**?

3 What fraction of these rabbits are **white**?

4 Circle **one quarter** of these birds.
Then fill in the blank in the sentence below.

One quarter of 8 is ☐.

Section Four — Fractions

Fractions of Amounts

5 Find $\frac{1}{3}$ of this set of 12 basketballs.

6 What is $\frac{3}{4}$ of 20?

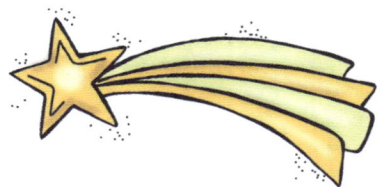

Colour in the stars below to help you.

7 Omar has 16 books. He gives $\frac{1}{4}$ of them to Helen.

How many books does he give to Helen?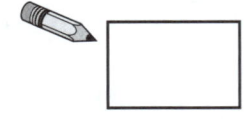

How many books does he have left?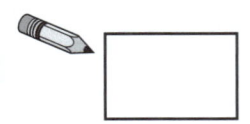

"I can work out simple fractions of amounts."

Equivalent Fractions

Warm Up Question

$\frac{1}{2}$ is the same as $\frac{?}{4}$. What is the missing number?
Use the dots on the right to help you.

1) Join up each shape with the fraction that is shaded.

$\frac{3}{4}$ $\frac{1}{4}$ $\frac{1}{2}$

2) Look at the number line below.

$3\frac{1}{4}$ $3\frac{2}{4}$ A   4 $4\frac{1}{4}$ B $4\frac{3}{4}$ 5

$3\frac{1}{2}$

What fraction goes in box A?

Write down **two** fractions that could go in box B.

                         or

"I can recognise equivalent fractions."

Progress Test 2

1 Allanah writes down the number 861.

What is this number in words?

[   ]

Partition the number 861 into hundreds, tens and ones.

861 = [   ] + [   ] + [   ]

2 marks

2 Join the pairs of numbers that add up to **100**.

20	0
90	40
60	80
50	10
100	50

2 marks

3 Put a tick next to each calculation that equals 20.

4 × 5 [ ]   2 × 10   [ ]

24 ÷ 2 [ ]   10 × 2   [ ]

5 × 5 [ ]   120 ÷ 10 [ ]

2 marks

Progress Test 2

4 What fraction of each shape is shaded?

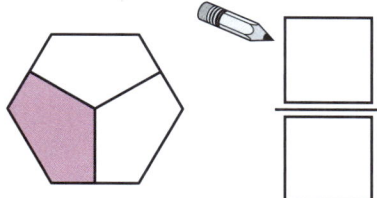 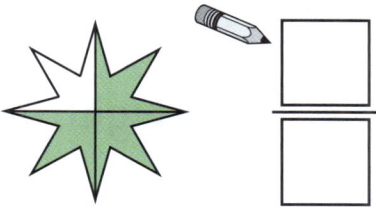

2 marks

5 Kofi has 45 stickers and Holly has 14 stickers.

How many stickers do they have in total?

How many more stickers does Kofi have than Holly?

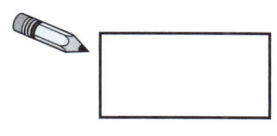

2 marks

6 Four friends each put six plums in the same box.

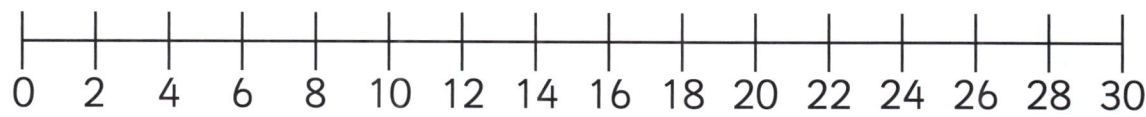

Use the number line to help you work out how many plums are in the box.

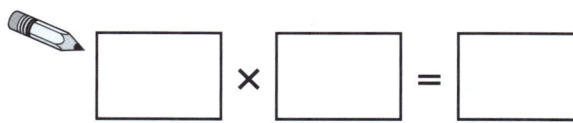

1 mark

Score: ☐/11

Section Five — Measurement

Units

1 Circle the correct unit of measurement for each object.

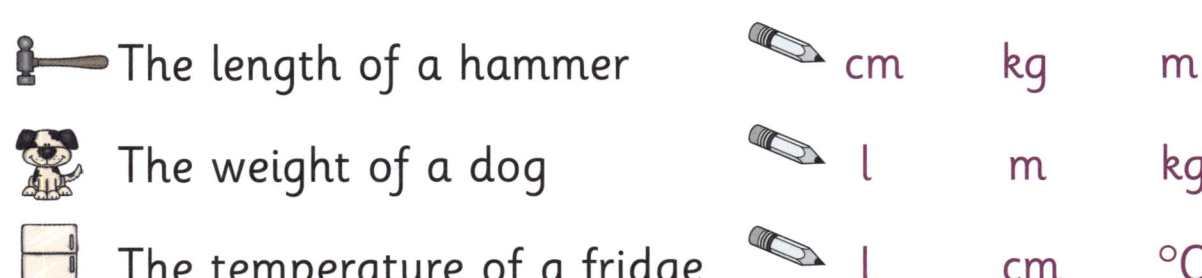

The length of a hammer	cm	kg	m
The weight of a dog	l	m	kg
The temperature of a fridge	l	cm	°C

2 Fill in the gaps using the correct units from the list below.

| g | cm | °C | kg | ml | m | l |

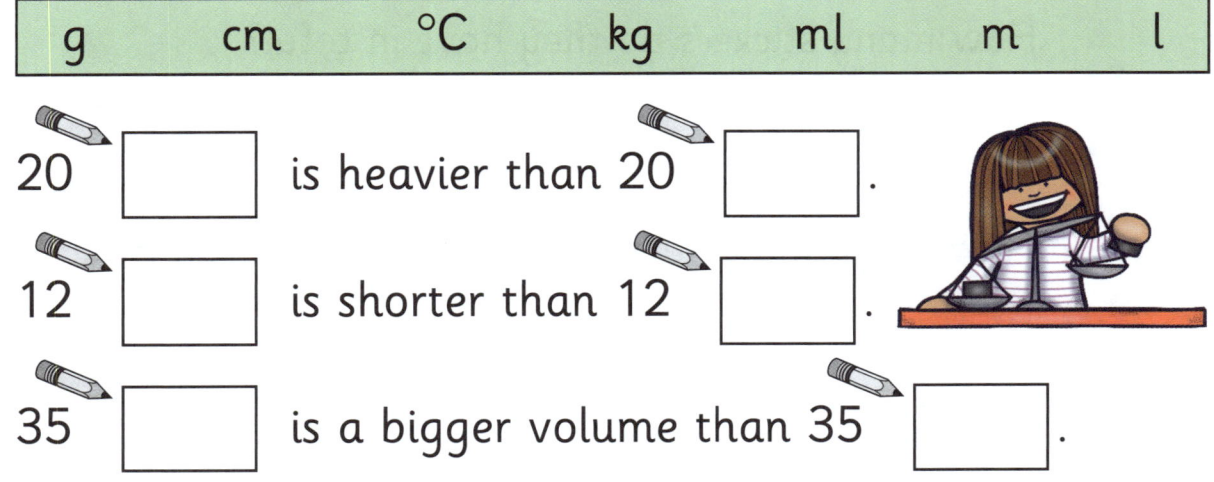

20 ☐ is heavier than 20 ☐.

12 ☐ is shorter than 12 ☐.

35 ☐ is a bigger volume than 35 ☐.

3 Draw a line to match each animal to its length.

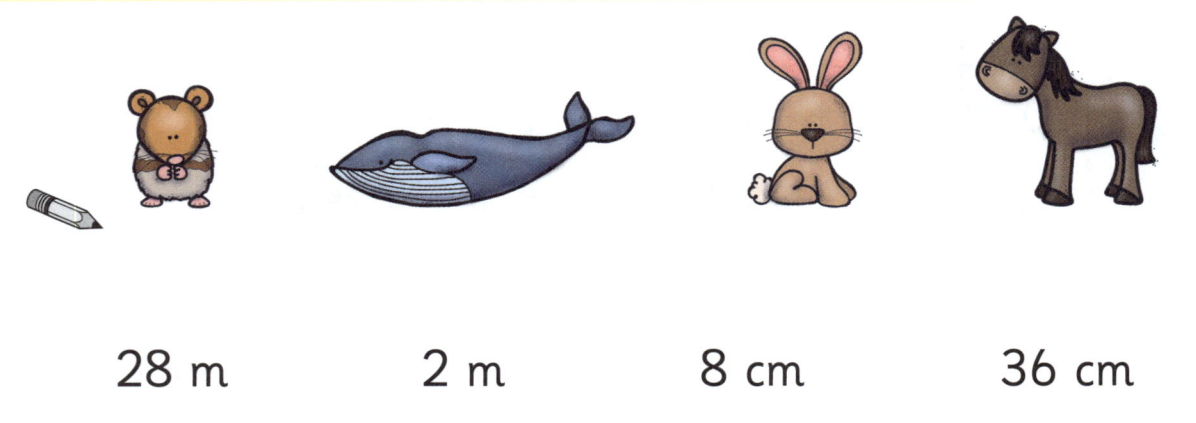

28 m   2 m   8 cm   36 cm

"I can estimate length, height, mass, volume and temperature using the correct units."

Measuring

1 Circle the best measuring tool for each task.

Pippa wants to measure 100 ml of juice.

Jake wants to find out how hot it is outside.

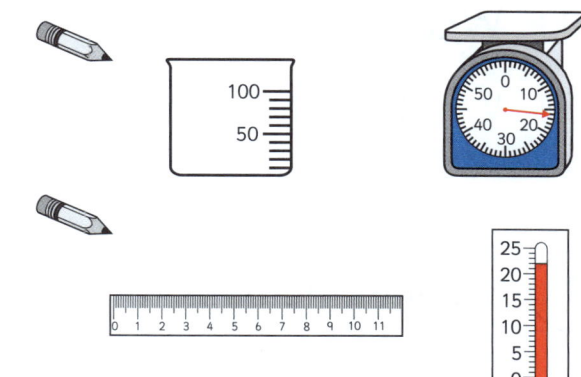

2 Write down the temperature of each object.

3 Draw a line to show the correct volume of water in each container.

35 ml:

60 ml:

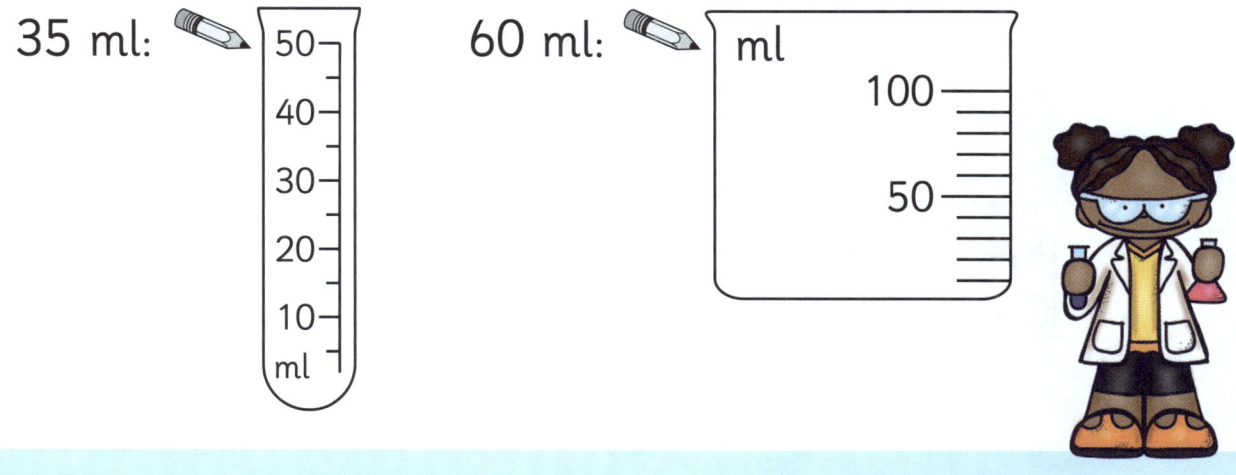

"I can use the right tools to measure length, height, mass, volume and temperature."

Section Five — Measurement

Comparing Measurements

> **Warm Up Questions**
>
> 1) Which of these objects is **lightest**?   7 g
> 2) Which of these objects is **heaviest**?   10 g   22 g

1   Fill in the gaps to make the number sentences **true**.

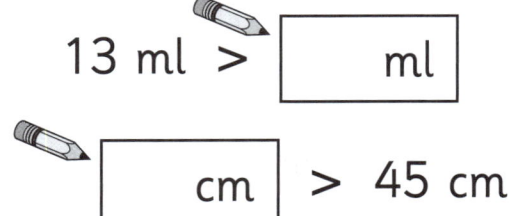

2   The items below are in order from **heaviest** to **lightest**. Match each item to its weight. One has been done for you.

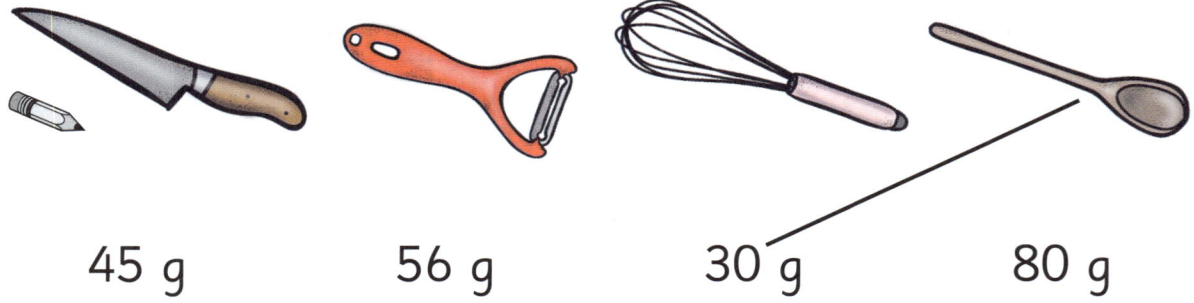

45 g   56 g   30 g   80 g

3   A green crayon is **half as long** as this orange crayon.

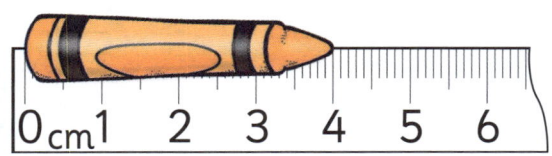

How long is the green crayon?

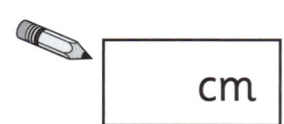 cm

"I can compare and order length, mass and volume."

Money

1 Write the missing amounts on the coins to make all the coins in each box add up to 60p.

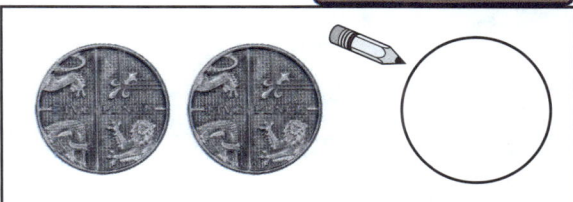

2 Add up **all** the coins below.

£ [ ] and [ ] p

3 Find **two** more ways to make 30p using these coins.

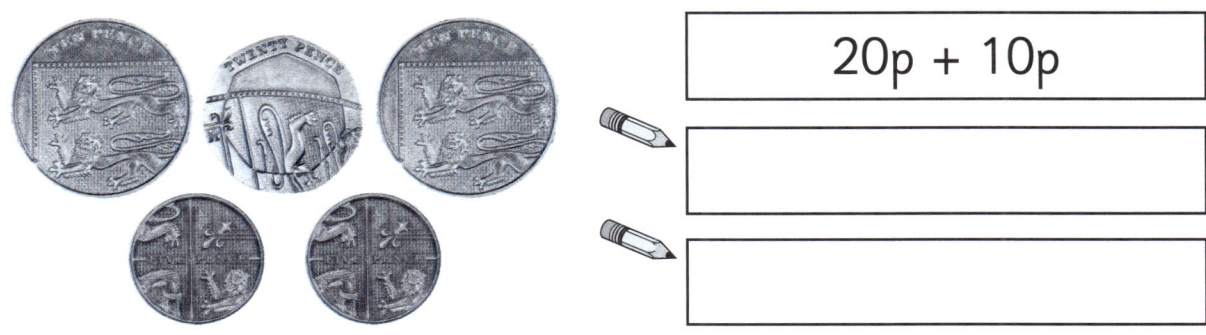

20p + 10p

"I can use pounds (£) and pence (p) to make up different amounts of money."

Section Five — Measurement

Sums with Money

1) Joe has **£1** to spend at the shop. Here is his shopping list.

Milk   40p
Snack bar   25p
Apple   30p

Work out the total cost of all the items on Joe's list.

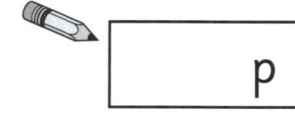 p

Does Joe have enough money?

 Yes ☐ No ☐

2) Ida has 80p. A ride at the funfair costs 85p.

Ida's mum gives her this coin:
How much money
does Ida have now?

 p

Ida uses all of her money to pay for the ride.
How much **change** does she get?

 p

3) AJ buys a yo-yo with the coins below and gets 10p change.

How much does the yo-yo cost?

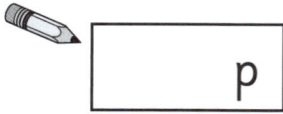 p

"I can add and subtract money to give change."

Section Five — Measurement

Time

1 Use some of the words below to give the time on each clock.

| quarter five to past half four |

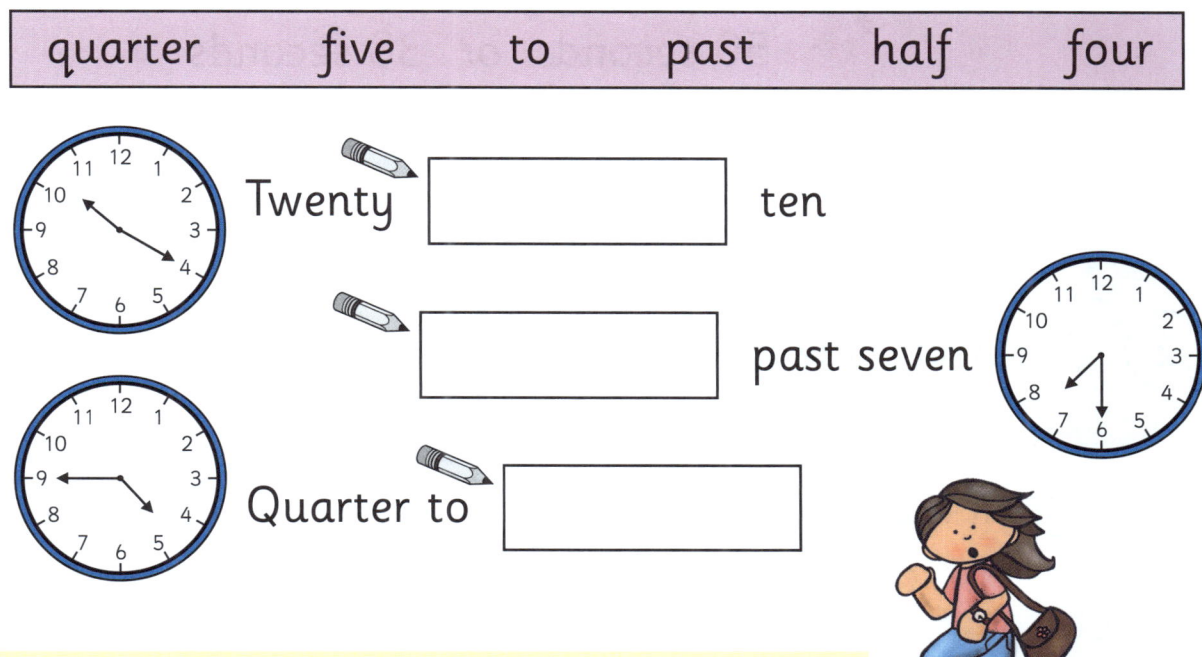

Twenty [_____] ten

[_____] past seven

Quarter to [_____]

2 Draw the missing hand on each clock face.

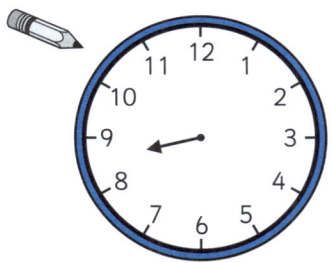 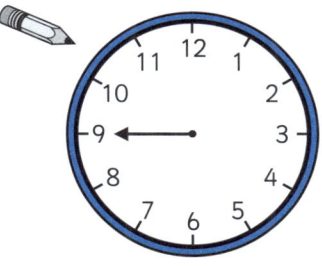 

Half past eight   Quarter to one   Ten to twelve

3 Draw the hands on each clock face to show the correct time.

Twenty-five past three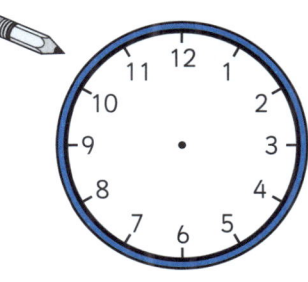

Five to nine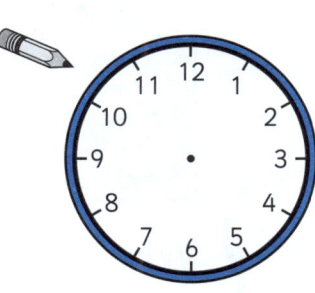

"I can tell the time and draw hands on a clock face to show time."

Section Five — Measurement

Comparing Time

1 Underline the **shorter** time in each pair.

- 50 seconds or 38 seconds
- 6 minutes or 8 minutes
- 2 minutes 12 seconds or 3 minutes

2 Look at these times from an obstacle race.

Put the racers in order from **quickest** to **slowest**.

Jean: 1 minute 30 seconds
Ibi: 1 minute 12 seconds
Ana: 2 minutes 5 seconds
Bel: 57 seconds

quickest ⟶ slowest

3 In a skipping rope competition the **longest** time wins. The four times are shown below.

Ali: 9 minutes 40 seconds
Sean: 8 minutes 17 seconds
Mick: 7 minutes
Dave: 8 minutes 35 seconds

Who won the competition?

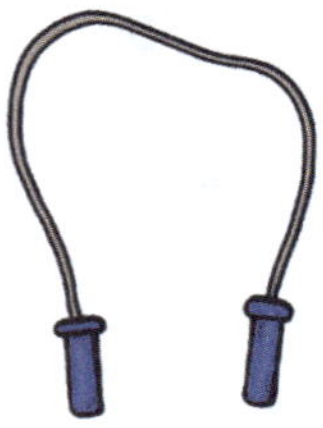

Who finished in third place?

"I can compare different lengths of time."

Section Five — Measurement

Section Six — Geometry

Flat (2D) Shapes

1) Jenna's shape has **4 equal sides** and **4 right angles**. Draw Jenna's shape in the box, then finish the sentence.

Jenna's shape is a _____.

2) Fill in the gaps using the words below.

| pentagon | quadrilateral | hexagon | octagon |

A _____ has **five** sides.

A _____ has **six** sides.

An _____ has **eight** sides.

3) Tick the pictures that show a **line of symmetry**.

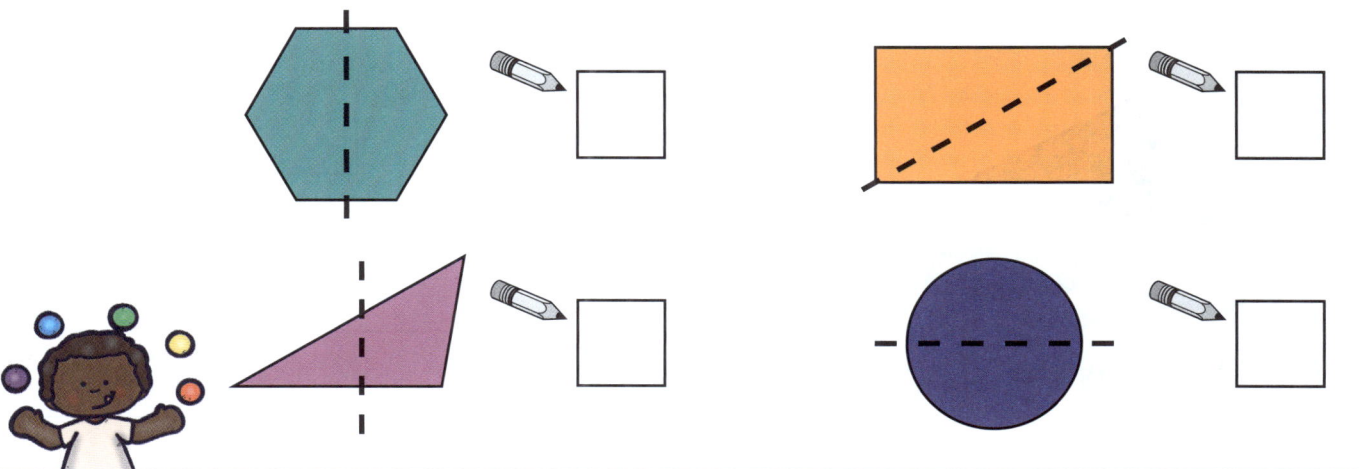

"I can draw and describe 2D shapes."

Solid (3D) Shapes

1 Match each shape to its name.

Sphere   Cuboid   Cylinder   Cone

2 Draw the shape inside the box. Then write down how many faces it has. The first shape has been drawn for you.

Square-based pyramid

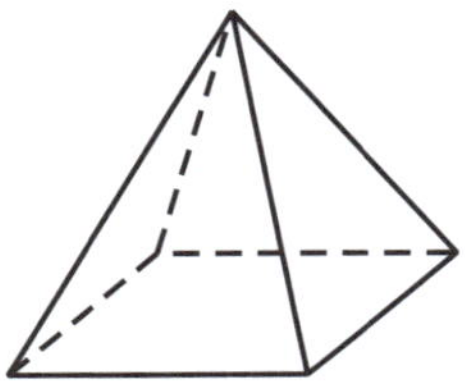

[ ] faces

Cube

[ ] faces

3 Count how many faces, edges and vertices this shape has.

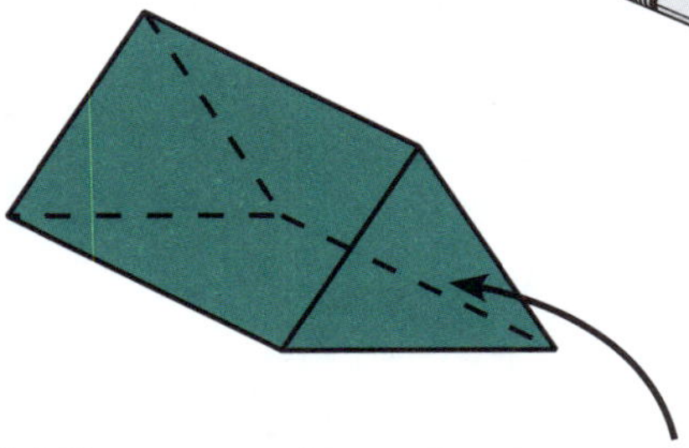

[ ] faces   [ ] edges

[ ] vertices

What is the shape of this face? [ ]

"I can draw and describe 3D shapes."

Sorting Shapes

1 Tick the shape that has more sides.

2 Circle the shape below that could not be sorted into either box.

| Four sides | Five sides |

3 Circle all the objects that are spheres.

"I can compare and sort 2D and 3D shapes and everyday objects."

Section Six — Geometry

Drawing Shapes and Patterns

Warm Up Questions

1) Which of the patterns on the right are symmetrical? Explain how you know.

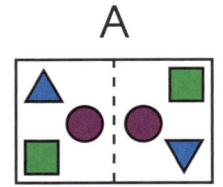 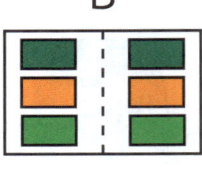 

2) Describe the sequence below in words.

1 Describe the pattern on the arrow. The first one has been done for you.

Purple and blue squares

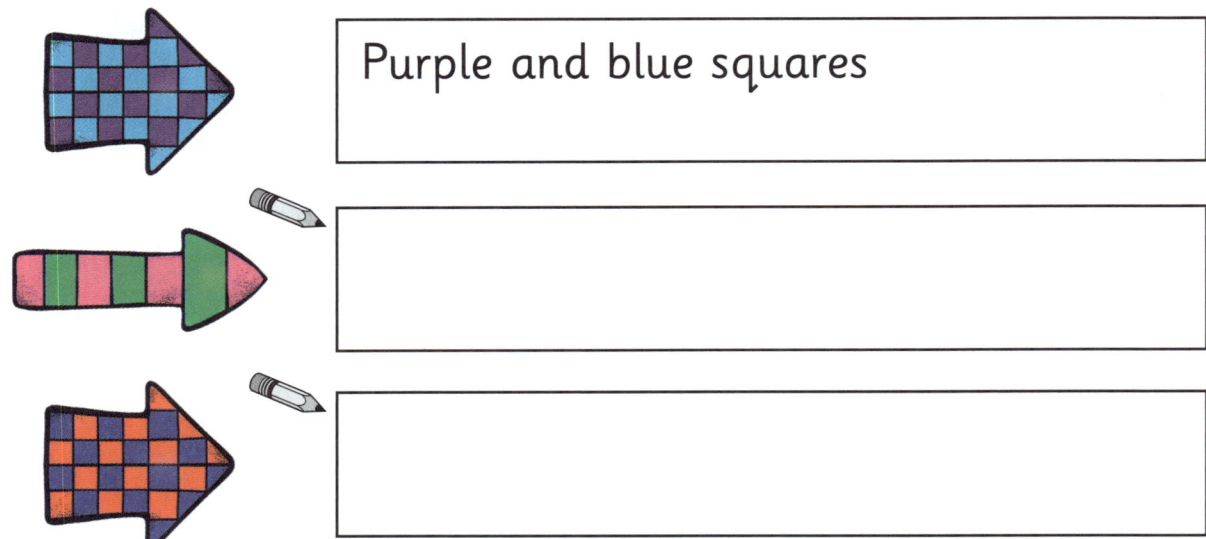

2 Draw **two** more shapes to make the pattern symmetrical.

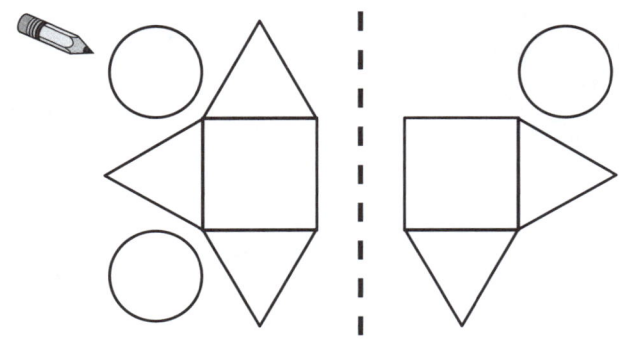 

Section Six — Geometry

Drawing Shapes and Patterns

3 Colour the picture to make the two butterflies symmetrical.

4 Tick the two shapes that come next in this sequence.

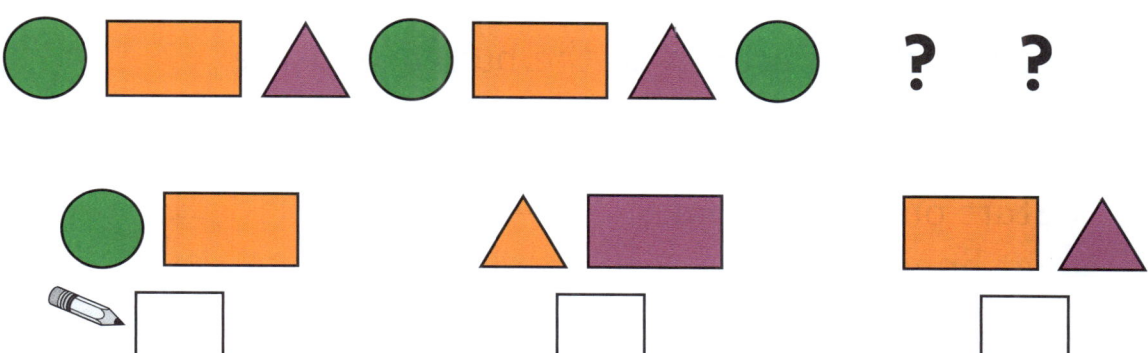

5 Write down the number of sides of each shape in this sequence.

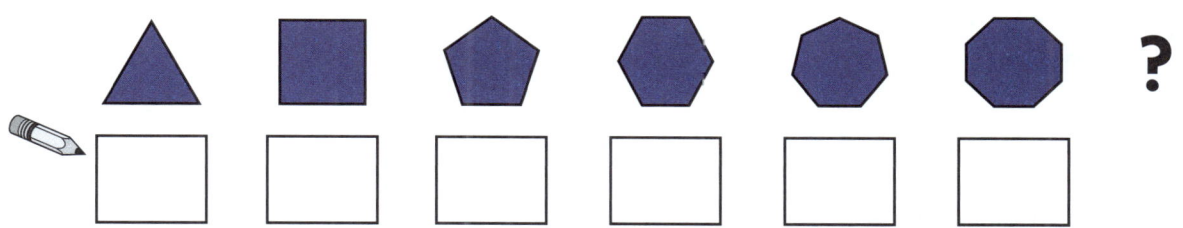

How many sides will the next shape have?

"I can recognise and make patterns and sequences out of shapes."

Position

1 Fill in the gaps with the words below to describe where the objects are on the grid.

| top | left | bottom | right |

The **bus** is in the [ ] [ ] -hand square.

The **car** is in the [ ] [ ] -hand square.

2 Follow the directions to the buried treasure. Mark an **X** on the map where you finish.

Start on the bottom left-hand square.

Go right 4 squares towards the tree, then go up 1 square.

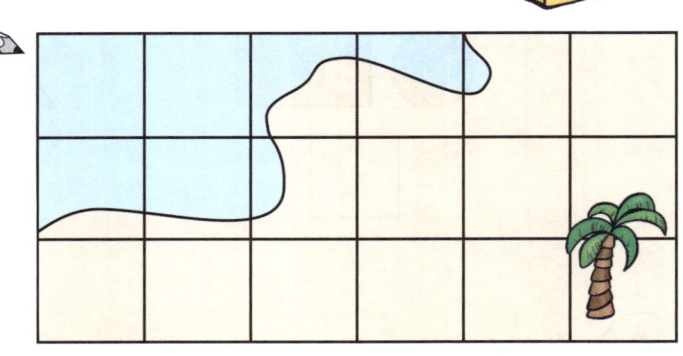

3 Circle the right words to describe the journey from **A** to **B**.

Go forwards, then take the **first** / **second** left.

Go forwards, then turn **left** / **right**.

Finally go **forwards** / **left** towards B.

"I can describe position and movement."

Section Six — Geometry

Direction and Turns

1) Mark all the **right angles** inside these shapes. One has been done for you.

2) Fill in the gaps using the words below.

| quarter | four | three | half | two | whole |

There are ⬚ right angles in a half turn.

A quarter turn clockwise is the same as a ⬚-quarter turn anticlockwise.

There are four right angles in a ⬚ turn.

3) A turtle spins around. It makes the turns below. Tick the box to show the direction it ends up facing.

A **three-quarter** turn **clockwise**.

Then a **half** turn **anticlockwise**.

Then a **quarter** turn **clockwise**.

"I know what a right angle is, and how many are in a quarter, half and three-quarter turn."

Section Six — Geometry

Progress Test 3

1 Circle all of the shapes that have $\frac{1}{3}$ shaded.

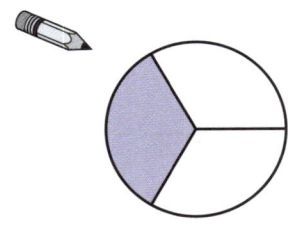 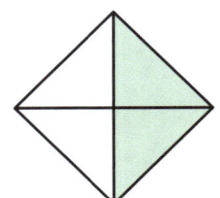 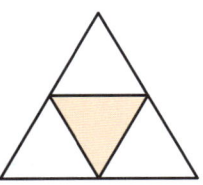 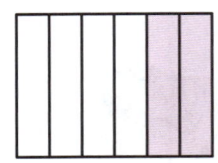

1 mark

2 The fastest time in an egg and spoon race gets 1st place.

Put these times in order from **1st place** to **4th place**.

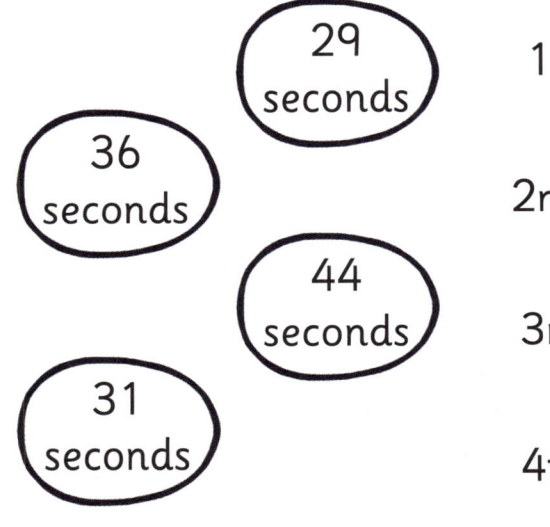

1st:  seconds

2nd: _____ seconds

3rd:  seconds

4th:  seconds

2 marks

3 Write a subtraction you could use to check the answer to 33 + 45 = 78.

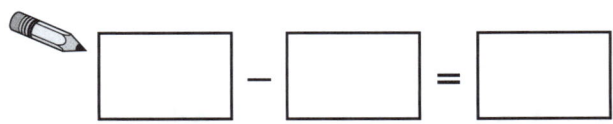

1 mark

Progress Test 3

4 Colour all the pentagons blue and all the hexagons red.

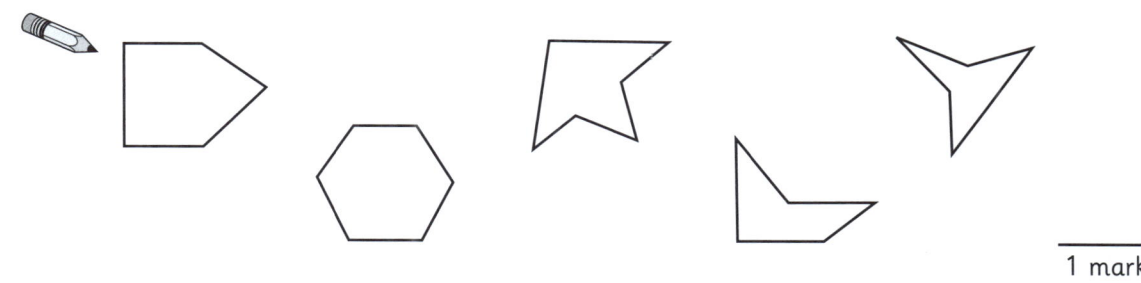

1 mark

5 Draw a line to match each measuring tool to its unit.

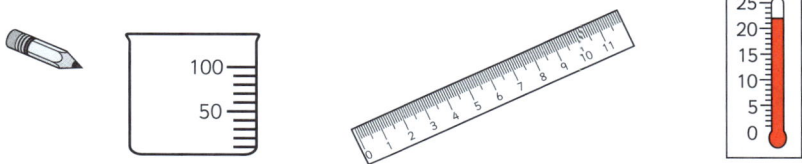

°C   g   ml   cm

2 marks

6 Colour in $\frac{3}{4}$ of this set of 8 cats.

Use the pictures to work out $\frac{3}{4}$ of 8.

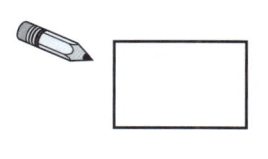

1 mark

Progress Test 3

7 Write down the weight of this egg.

☐ g

1 mark

8 Start at point **A** and follow the instructions below. Which letter do you end up at?

Go forwards, then make a quarter turn anticlockwise.
Go forwards, then make a quarter turn clockwise.
Go backwards out of the maze.

☐

1 mark

9 Fill in the gaps using the words and numbers below.

| circle | pyramid | prism | square | 5 | 7 | 4 | 8 |

This is a ☐.

Four of its faces are triangles and the other face is a ☐.

It has ☐ edges and ☐ vertices.

2 marks

Progress Test 3

10) Udoka has 39 T-shirts on his market stall.
He sells 24 of them. How many does he have left?

_____
1 mark

11) Use the number line to work out these divisions.

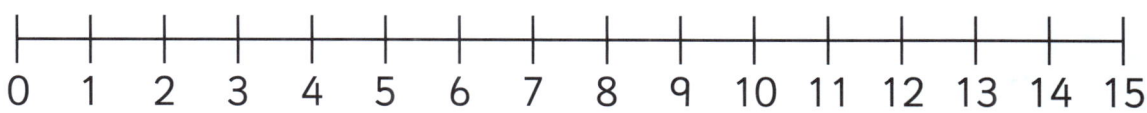

15 ÷ 3

_____
1 mark

12 ÷ 4

_____
1 mark

12) Ian uses a **£1** coin to pay for a drink.
He gets these coins as change.

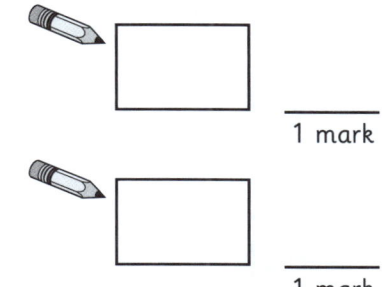

How much did Ian's drink cost?

p _____
1 mark

What other coins could he have
been given for the same change?

_____
1 mark

Score: ____/17

Section Seven — Statistics

Tables

1 Five friends drew their favourite animals in this table.

	Mara	Will	Adil	Penny	Eleni
Favourite animal	🐶	🐰	🐱	🐶	🐱

How many people said their favourite animal was:

a cat?    a rabbit?

2 Draw a table to show the number of each fruit shown on the right.

3 The table shows the colours of some cars in a car park.

How many black cars were there?

How many more white cars than blue cars were there?

	Number of cars
Red	15
Blue	11
White	21
Black	16

"I can draw and use simple tables."

Tally Charts

Warm Up Question

Lucia counted the number of eggs laid by some chickens and made this tally: |||| |||| |||

How many eggs does this represent?

1 Tamsin counted the flowers that she saw on her walk.

Fill in the missing parts of Tamsin's tally chart.

Flower	Tally	Total
Rose		15
Buttercup	|||| |||| ||	
Daffodil	|||| |||| |||| ||	
Daisy		8

Which flower did she see the most of?

2 Fill in this tally chart with the number of red, yellow and blue blocks in the tower.

Colour	Tally	Total
Red		
Yellow		
Blue		

"I can answer questions using a tally chart."

Section Seven — Statistics

Block Diagrams

1 Mr Maynard asked his class what they would like to do in Music. The results are shown in the block diagram.

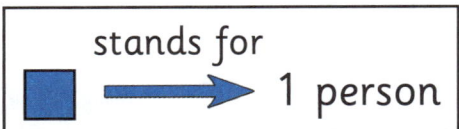 stands for 1 person

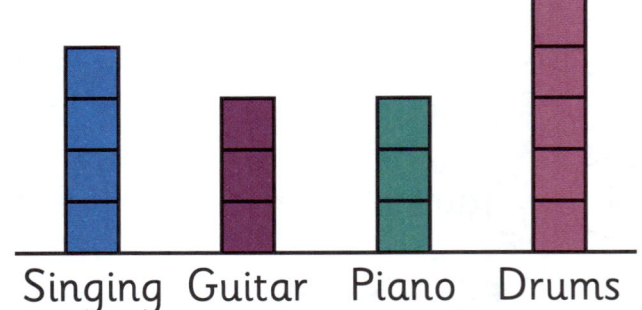

Which option was the most popular?

How many more pupils said drums than piano?

How many pupils were asked in total?

2 Use the table to finish the block diagram. One has been done for you.

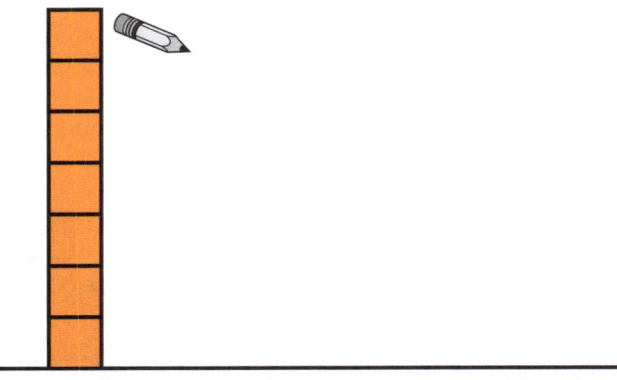
Brown Blonde Ginger Black

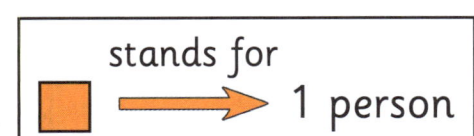 stands for 1 person

Hair colour	Number
Brown	7
Blonde	4
Ginger	5
Black	3

"I can answer questions using a block diagram."

Section Seven — Statistics

Pictograms

1 This pictogram shows the number of trees in four parks. Henwater has 7 trees. Add this to the pictogram.

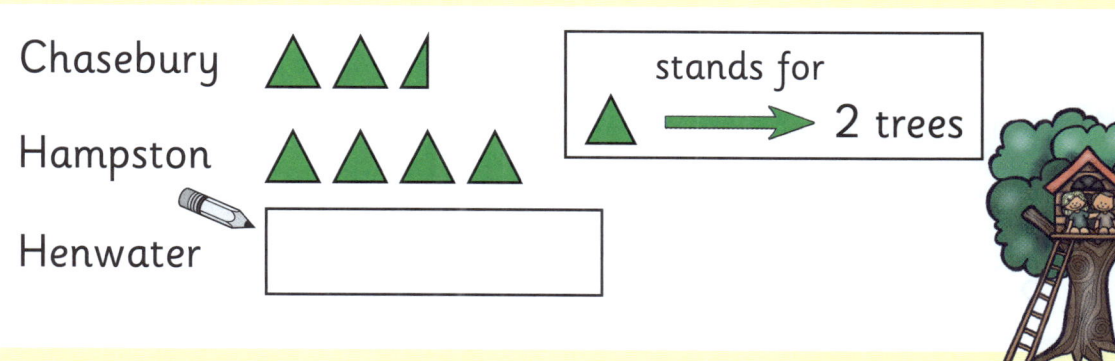

2 Three Year 2 classes played some games on Sports Day. The pictogram shows how many points they got.

Which class got the most points?

Class ▢

How many fewer points did class 2A get than class 2B?

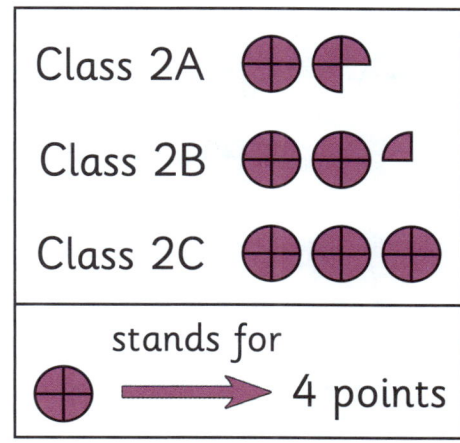

3 Erica and her friends ate some strawberries. Erica ate 5 strawberries, Kai ate 3 and Damian ate 4.

Use this information to finish the pictogram. One has been done for you.

Erica ♥ ♥ ❥

Kai

Damian

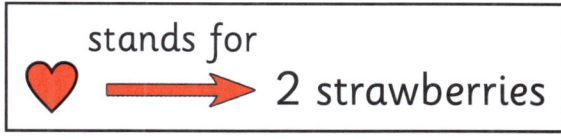

"I can draw and use pictograms."

Section Seven — Statistics

Year Two Objectives Test

1 **Estimate** the number on this number line.

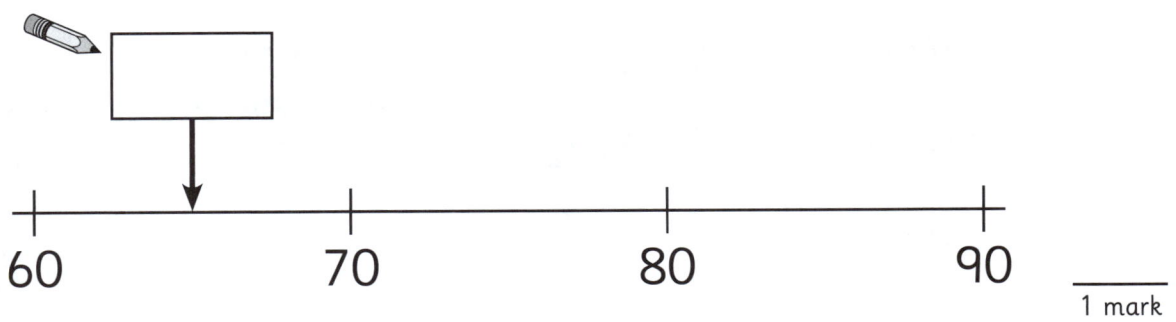

1 mark

2 Aiko wants to work out 3 × 6. Write down a **repeated addition** she could use to find the answer.

[ ] = [ ]

1 mark

3 Look at the shape below.

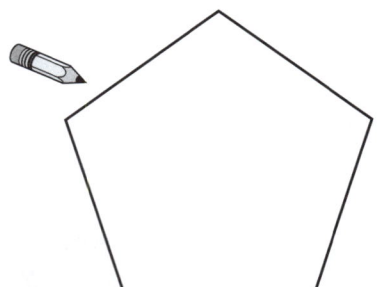

What is the name of this shape?

Using a ruler, draw a line of symmetry onto the shape.

2 marks

Year Two Objectives Test

4 Circle the numbers that are both even **and** in the five times table.

10   15   12   20

8   45   30

_____
1 mark

5 Shade in $\frac{3}{4}$ of the shape below.

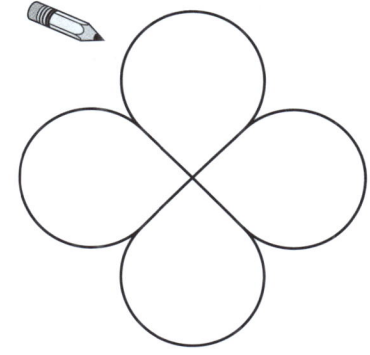

_____
1 mark

6 Write the correct number from the list below in each box.

| 39 | 37 | 43 |

38 > ☐   41 < ☐

30 + 9 = ☐

_____
2 marks

Year Two Objectives Test

7 Tick the box below each clock that shows 'quarter to'.

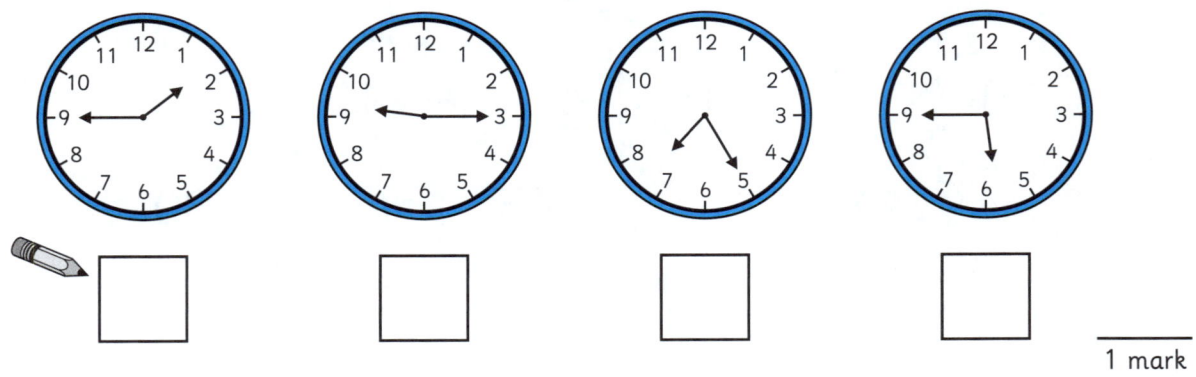

1 mark

8 Kimberly has 9 toy pigs.
She gives $\frac{1}{3}$ of them to a friend.

How many toy pigs does Kimberly give away?

1 mark

9 Rob has the following coins to spend at a shop.

Rob spends 60p. How much money does he have left?

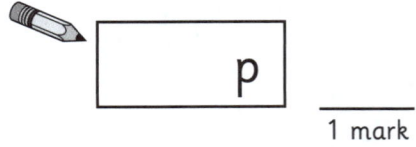

1 mark

Year Two Objectives Test

10 Leo has 23 model trains and 34 model planes. How many more planes than trains does Leo have?

1 mark

11 Colour the picture to make the next shape in the sequence.

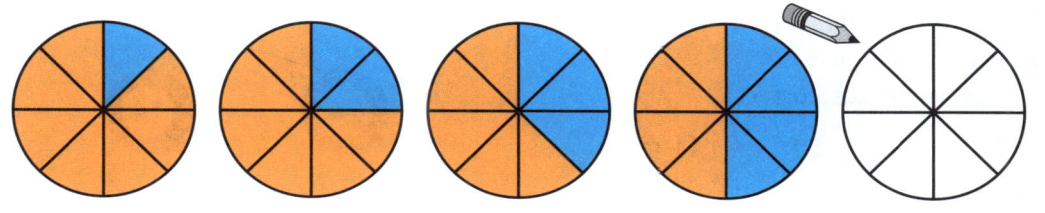

1 mark

12 Some people were asked to choose their favourite sport. The pictogram below shows the results.

7 people chose cricket. Show this on the pictogram.

   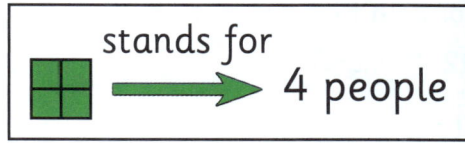

How many more people chose football than rugby?

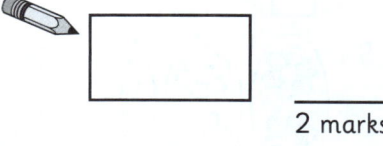

2 marks

Score: ☐ /15

Answers

Pages 2-5 — Year One Objectives Test

1)  (1 mark)

2) **8 cm** (1 mark)
   The pencil is longer / (shorter) than the pen. (1 mark)

3) **17** (1 mark)

4)
   (1 mark for both cubes circled)

5) There are **7** days in a week.
   There are **31** days in August.
   (1 mark for both sentences correct)

6) 1 (8) 5 7 (2) 4 (1 mark)
   3 + **17** = 20 (1 mark)

7) ▢ (1 mark)

8) 19 – 3 = **16** (1 mark)
   The difference between 11 and 17 is **6**. (1 mark)

9)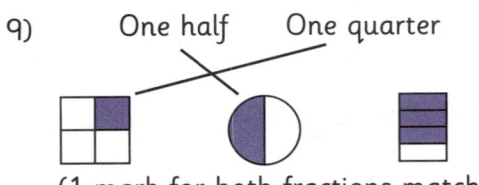
   (1 mark for both fractions matched)

10) 2 × 6 = **12** (1 mark)

11) ✓ (1 mark)

12) E.g.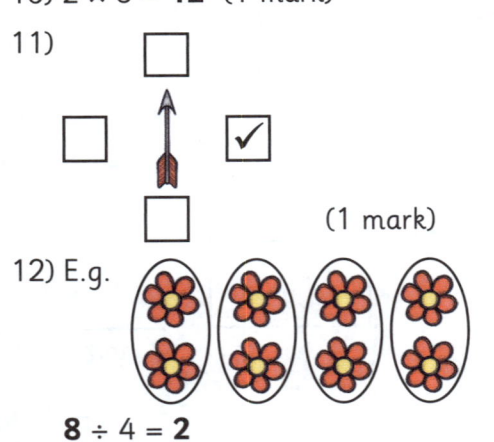
    8 ÷ 4 = **2**
    (1 mark for both numbers correct)

Section One — Number and Place Value

Page 6 — Place Value

1) 43 has **4** tens and **3** ones.
   89 has **8** tens and **9** ones.

2) **1** Ten, **7** Ones, **17**
   2 Tens, **5** Ones, **25**

3) **87** is the biggest 2-digit number you can make.

Page 7 — Numbers to 100

Warm Up: 17 — "**Seventeen**"
54 — "**Fifty-four**"
90 — "**Ninety**"

1)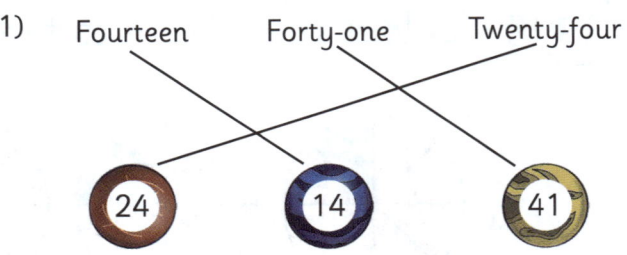

2) Eleven — **11**
   Fifty-five — **55**
   Thirty-nine — **39**
   One hundred and ten — **110**

3) 22 — **Twenty-two**
   98 — **Ninety-eight**

Page 8 — Twos, Threes, Fives and Tens

1)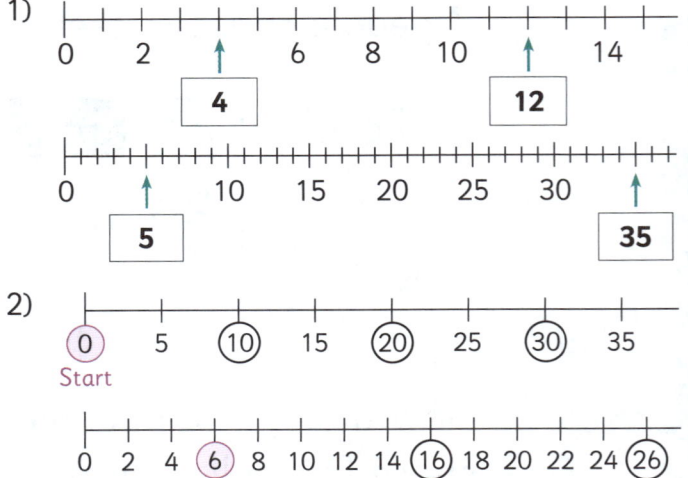

2) (number line with 0 Start, (10), 15, (20), 25, (30), 35)
   (number line 0, 2, 4, (6) Start, 8, 10, 12, 14, (16), 18, 20, 22, 24, (26))

3) 3, 6, 9, **12**
   53, 43, 33, **23**

Answers

Answers

Page 9 — The Number Line

1)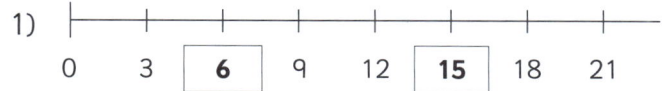

2)

3) E.g.
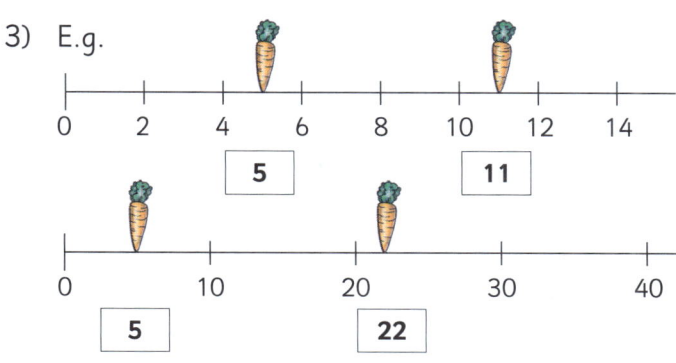

Page 10 — Partitioning

Warm Up 1: **63** has 3 ones.

Warm Up 2: **81** has 8 tens.

1)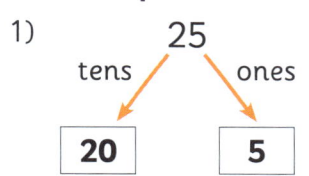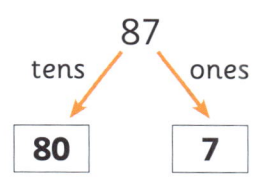

2) 11 = 10 + 2 ✗   89 = 70 + 19 ✓
   76 = 30 + 46 ✓   96 = 60 + 9 ✗

3) E.g. 45 = **40 + 5**
   45 = **20 + 25**

Page 11 — Ordering and Comparing Numbers

1) 6   22   12   (24)
   (55)   50   54   45

2) **26, 27, 43, 47**

3) E.g.

4) 77 > 23
   3 + 2 = 5
   37 < 79

Pages 12-13 — Solving Number Problems

1) Noah has 5 + 3 = **8** pets.
2) There are 6 − 2 = **4** cats left on the wall.
3) There are 10 + 7 = **17** birds in Sadie's garden.
4) Muhammad has 30 − 4 = **26** oranges left.
5) Gwen delivers 22 + 10 = **32** letters.
6) There are 48 − 20 = **28** books left.

Pages 14-15 — Progress Test 1

1) **97** is the biggest 2-digit number you can make. (1 mark)
   45 is the smallest 2-digit number you can make. (1 mark)

2) 31 — **Thirty-one** (1 mark)
   75 — **Seventy-five** (1 mark)
   108 — **One hundred and eight** (1 mark)

3)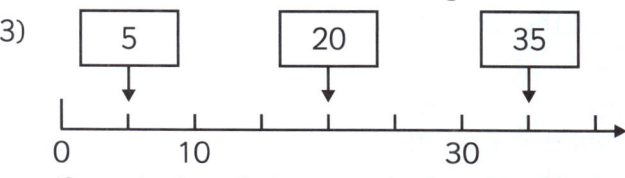
   (2 marks for all three numbers correct, otherwise 1 mark for at least one number correct)

4) Any two correct partitionings,
   e.g. 94 = **90 + 4**
   94 = **80 + 10 + 4**
   (1 mark for each correct partitioning)

5) There are 43 − 10 = **33** grapes left. (1 mark)

6) 42 < 68 (1 mark)
   3 + 7 > 11 − 2 (1 mark)

7) They make 50 + 29 = **79** cupcakes. (1 mark)

Section Two — Addition and Subtraction

Page 16 — Number Bonds

1)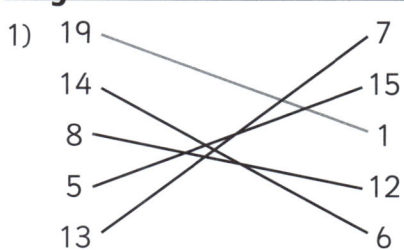

Answers

2) **17 − 12 = 5** or **17 − 5 = 12**

3)

Pages 17-18 — Adding

Warm Up: If you add enough ones, you can change the digit in the tens place. For example, adding 2 ones to 18 gives 20. This has a different digit in the tens place (2) than 18 (1).

1) 37 + 2 ones / (**tens**) = 57 (37 + 20 = 57)
   62 + 3 (**ones**) / tens = 65 (62 + 3 = 65)

2) 20 + 50 = **70**   1 + 6 = **7**
   70 + 7 = **77** (or **7 + 70 = 77**)

3) 48 + 23 = **71**
   59 + 19 = **78**

4) 41 = 40 + 1
   Add the tens: 40 + 30 = 70
   70 + 1 = 71, so 41 + 30 = **71**

   25 = 20 + 5, 32 = 30 + 2
   Add the tens: 20 + 30 = 50
   Add the ones: 5 + 2 = 7
   50 + 7 = 57, so 25 + 32 = **57**

   76 = 70 + 6, 14 = 10 + 4
   70 + 10 = 80, 6 + 4 = 10
   80 + 10 = 90, so 76 + 14 = **90**

5) E.g. Using partitioning:
   43 = 40 + 3, 24 = 20 + 4
   Add the tens: 40 + 20 = 60
   Add the ones: 3 + 4 = 7
   They sell 60 + 7 = **67** jumpers in total.

6) E.g. Using partitioning:
   52 = 50 + 2, 39 = 30 + 9
   Add the tens: 50 + 30 = 80
   Add the ones: 2 + 9 = 11
   80 + 11 = 91, so there are now **91** sheep.

Pages 19-20 — Subtracting

1)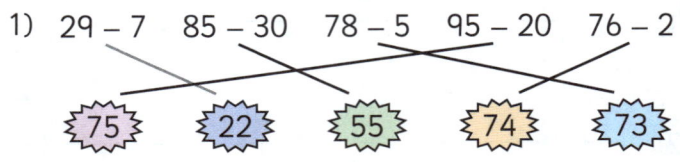

2) 49 = 40 + 9, 18 = 10 + 8
   Subtract the tens: 40 − 10 = 30
   Subtract the ones: 9 − 8 = 1
   30 + 1 = 31, so 49 − 18 = **31**

   58 = 50 + 8, 42 = 40 + 2
   50 − 40 = 10, 8 − 2 = 6
   10 + 6 = 16, so 58 − 42 = **16**

3) The difference between 37 and 61 is **24**.

4) 72 − 53 = **19**
   83 − 67 = **16**

5) E.g. Using partitioning:
   68 = 60 + 8, 13 = 10 + 3
   Subtract the tens: 60 − 10 = 50
   Subtract the ones: 8 − 3 = 5
   She has 50 + 5 = **55** seeds now.

6) E.g. Using partitioning:
   36 = 30 + 6, 24 = 20 + 4
   Subtract the tens: 30 − 20 = 10
   Subtract the ones: 6 − 4 = 2
   10 + 2 = 12, so Jack hit the ball **12** more times than Sue.

Page 21 — Checking

1) 25 + 22 = 47, so **25 + 22** should be circled.
   82 − 43 = 39, so **82 − 43** should be circled.

2) 34 + 19 − 19 = 19 ☐
   52 − 25 + 25 = 52 ✓
   66 + 31 − 31 = 66 ✓
   (34 + 19 − 19 = 34, not 19.)

3) Any one of these additions:
   1 + 6 + 8 = 15, **1 + 8 + 6 = 15**,
   8 + 6 + 1 = 15, **8 + 1 + 6 = 15**,
   6 + 8 + 1 = 15
   Any one of these subtractions:
   15 − 6 − 8 = 1, **15 − 8 − 6 = 1**,
   15 − 6 − 1 = 8, **15 − 1 − 6 = 8**,
   15 − 1 − 8 = 6, **15 − 8 − 1 = 6**

Answers

Section Three — Multiplication and Division

Pages 22-23 — Times Tables

Warm Up 1: **6**, **8**, **10**, **12**, **14**, **16**

Warm Up 2: 10, **15**, **20**, 25, **30**

1)

2) 7 × 2 = **14**   11 × 2 = **22**
   6 × 5 = **30**   12 × 5 = **60**
   8 × 10 = **80**   9 × 10 = **90**

3) **32** or **34**

4)

5)

Number	Odd or Even?	Times Table
8	Even	② 5 10
45	**Odd**	2 ⑤ 10
24	**Even**	② 5 10
20	**Even**	② ⑤ ⑩

Page 24 — Using Times Tables Facts

1) **10 × 9 = 90**
   2 × 11 = 22

2) (10 × 8)   6 × 10   6 × 5
       2 × 8   (8 × 10)

3) 35 ÷ 5 = **7**   35 ÷ 7 = **5**
   50 ÷ 10 = **5**   50 ÷ 5 = **10**

Page 25 — Multiplying

1) 3 × 8 = **24**

2) Count right in 3 groups of 4, e.g.

   [number line from 0 to 15 with jumps of 4]

   3 × 4 = **12**

3)

Multiplication	Repeated Addition	Answer
2 × 3	3 + 3	6
5 × 3	3 + 3 + 3 + 3 + 3 (or **5 + 5 + 5**)	**15**
3 × 3	3 + 3 + 3	**9**
4 × 3	3 + 3 + 3 + 3 (or **4 + 4 + 4**)	**12**

Page 26 — Dividing

1) E.g.

   18 ÷ 3 = **6**

2) Count right in 2s until you reach 12, e.g.

   [number line from 0 to 12 with jumps of 2]

   12 ÷ 2 = **6**

3) 25 ÷ 5 = **5**

Page 27 — Double and Half

1)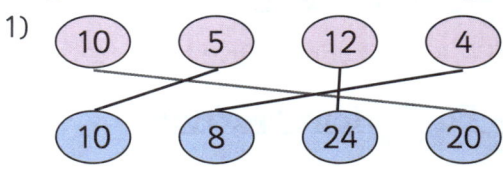

2) Half of 16 is **8**.   Double 12 is **24**.

3) Double 9 is **18** toads.

4) $\frac{1}{2}$ of 14 = **7** $\frac{1}{2}$ of 22 = **11**

Section Four — Fractions

Page 28 — Thirds and Quarters

1)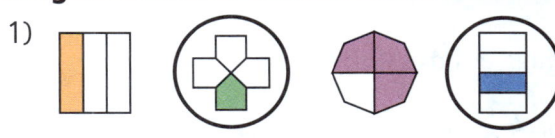

2) E.g. [shaded fraction diagrams]

3) One third of the circle is green. — **True**
   Three quarters of the rectangle is orange. — **False**

Answers

Answers

Pages 29-30 — Fractions of Amounts

1) **Any two beetles** should be coloured blue.

2) $\frac{1}{4}$ of the frogs are orange.

   $\frac{3}{4}$ of the frogs are blue.

3) $\frac{1}{3}$ of the rabbits are white.

4) E.g.

   One quarter of 8 is **2**.

5) Split the basketballs into three equal groups.

   E.g.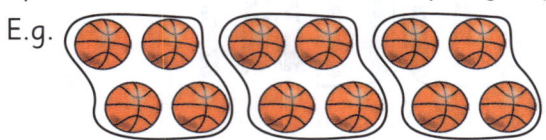

   $\frac{1}{3}$ of 12 basketballs is **4** basketballs.

6) E.g.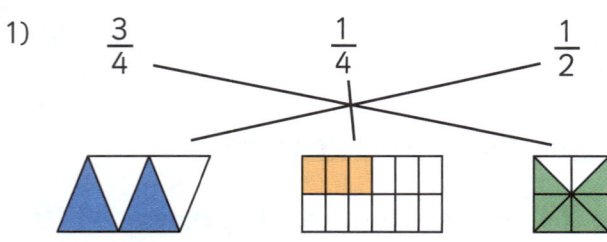

   $\frac{3}{4}$ of 20 = **15**.

7) He gives $\frac{1}{4}$ of 16 = **4** books to Helen.

   He has 16 − 4 = **12** books left.

Page 31 — Equivalent Fractions

Warm Up:
$\frac{1}{2}$ is the same as $\frac{2}{4}$, so this missing number is **2**.

1) $\frac{3}{4}$ — (rightmost shape, green eighths)
   $\frac{1}{4}$ — (middle shape, tenths grid)
   $\frac{1}{2}$ — (leftmost shape, blue triangles)

2) $3\frac{3}{4}$ goes in box A.

   $4\frac{2}{4}$ or $4\frac{1}{2}$ could go in box B.

Pages 32-33 — Progress Test 2

1) **Eight hundred and sixty-one** (1 mark)
   861 = **800** + **60** + **1** (1 mark)

2) 20 — 0
   90 — 40
   60 — 80
   50 — 10
   100 — 50
   (lines cross connecting to make 100)

   (2 marks for all lines correct, otherwise 1 mark for at least three lines correct)

3) 4 × 5 ✓   2 × 10 ✓
   24 ÷ 2   10 × 2 ✓
   5 × 5   120 ÷ 10

   (2 marks for all three ticked correctly with no others ticked, otherwise 1 mark for two ticked correctly and at most one ticked incorrectly)

4) $\frac{1}{3}$ (1 mark) $\frac{3}{4}$ (1 mark)

5) E.g. Using partitioning:
   45 = 40 + 5, 14 = 10 + 4
   Add the tens: 40 + 10 = 50
   Add the ones: 5 + 4 = 9
   50 + 9 = 59, so they have **59** stickers in total. (1 mark)
   E.g. Using partitioning:
   Subtract the tens: 40 − 10 = 30
   Subtract the ones: 5 − 4 = 1
   30 + 1 = 31, so Kofi has **31** more stickers than Holly. (1 mark)

6) Count right in 4 groups of 6, e.g.
   0 2 4 6 8 10 12 14 16 18 20 22 24 26 28 30

   4 × 6 = 24 (1 mark)

Section Five — Measurement

Page 34 — Units

1) It's a small length, so it's measured in **cm**.
   It's a weight, so it's measured in **kg**.
   It's a temperature, so it's measured in **°C**.

2) 20 **kg** is heavier than 20 g.
   12 **cm** is shorter than 12 m.
   35 **l** is a bigger volume than 35 ml.

Answers

3)
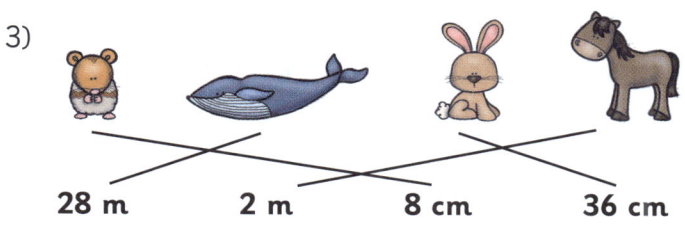

Page 35 — Measuring

1)
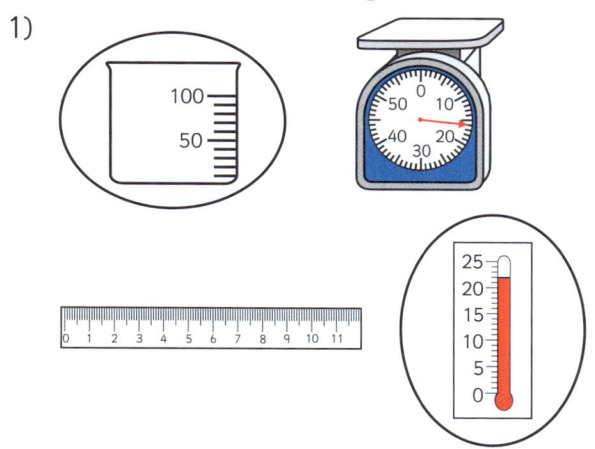

2) **10 °C**, **0 °C** and **24 °C**

3)
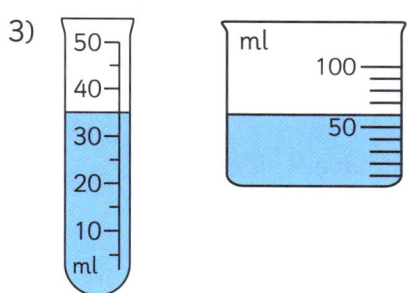

Page 36 — Comparing Measurements

Warm Up 1: 7 g is less than 10 g and 22 g, so the **pencil** is lightest.

Warm Up 2: 22 g is more than 10 g and 7 g, so the **glue stick** is heaviest.

1) Any number less than 13, e.g. 13 ml > **12** ml
   Any number more than 13, e.g. 13 °C < **15** °C
   Any number more than 45, e.g. **50 cm** > 45 cm
   2 l = 2 l

2)
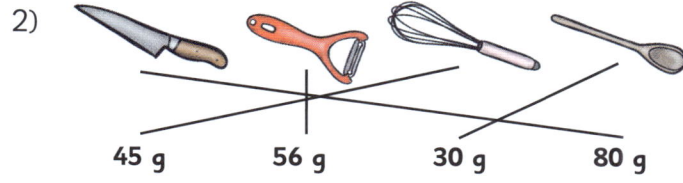

3) The orange crayon is 4 cm long.
   Half of 4 cm is 4 ÷ 2 = **2 cm**

Page 37 — Money

1)

2) £2 + 20p + 10p + 5p + 1p = **£2** and **36p**

3) **20p + 5p + 5p**
   10p + 10p + 5p + 5p

Page 38 — Sums with Money

1) 40p + 25p + 30p = **95p**
   Yes — £1 = 100p, which is more than 95p, so Joe does have enough money.

2) 80p + 20p = **100p**
   100p − 85p = **15p**

3) 50p + 5p + 20p = 75p
   75p − 10p = **65p**

Page 39 — Time

1) Twenty **past** ten
   Half past seven
   Quarter to **five**

2)

Half past eight Quarter to one Ten to twelve

3) Twenty-five past three:    Five to nine:

Page 40 — Comparing Time

1) **38 seconds** should be underlined.
   6 minutes should be underlined.
   2 minutes 12 seconds should be underlined.

2) **Bel, Ibi, Jean, Ana**

3) **Ali** won the competition.
   Sean finished in third place.

Answers

Answers

Section Six — Geometry

Page 41 — Flat (2D) Shapes

1) Jenna's shape is a **square**.

2) A **pentagon** has five sides.
A **hexagon** has six sides.
An **octagon** has eight sides.

3)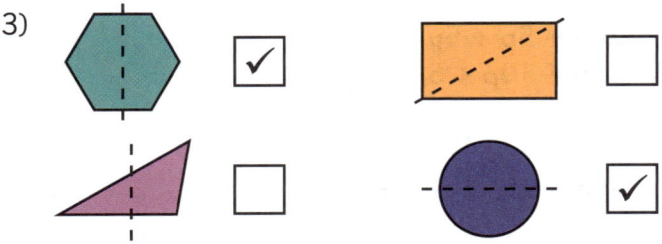

Page 42 — Solid (3D) Shapes

1)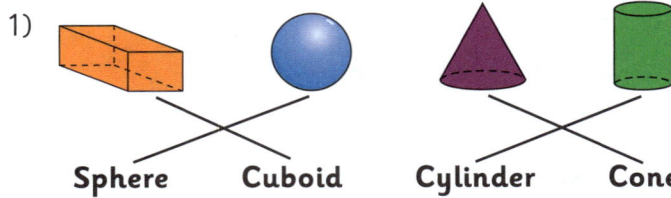

2) Square-based pyramid: **5** faces   Cube: **6** faces

3) **5** faces, **9** edges and **6** vertices
The face is a **triangle**.

Page 43 — Sorting Shapes

1)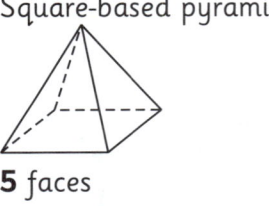

2) & 3)

Pages 44-45 — Drawing Shapes and Patterns

Warm Up 1: **B** and **C** are symmetrical.
E.g. If you fold each pattern along the mirror line, the two sides match.

Warm Up 2: E.g. A blue square, then a purple hexagon, then another blue square, then another purple hexagon, and so on.

1) **Green and pink (vertical) stripes**
Red and blue squares

2) & 3) & 4)

5) **3, 4, 5, 6, 7, 8**
The next shape will have **9** sides.

Page 46 — Position

1) The bus is in the **bottom left**-hand square.
The car is in the **top right**-hand square.

2)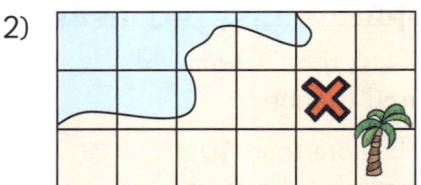

3) Go forwards then take the **first /(second)** left.
Go forwards, then turn **left /(right)**.
Finally go **(forwards)/ left** towards B.

Page 47 — Direction and Turns

1)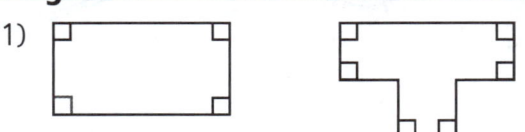

2) There are **two** right angles in a half turn.
A quarter turn clockwise is the same as a **three**-quarter turn anticlockwise.
There are four right angles in a **whole** turn.

Answers

3)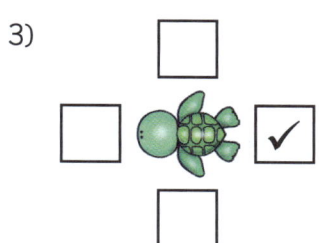

Pages 48-51 — Progress Test 3

1)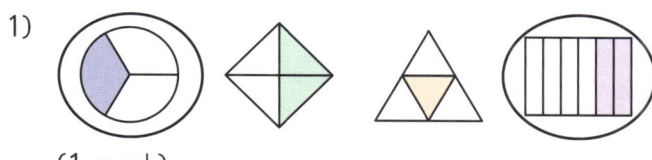
   (1 mark)

2) 1st: **29 seconds**
   2nd: **31 seconds**
   3rd: **36 seconds**
   4th: **44 seconds**
   (2 marks for all times correct, otherwise
   1 mark for at least two times correct)

3) **78 − 45 = 33** or **78 − 33 = 45** (1 mark)

4)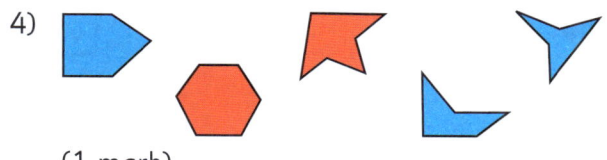
   (1 mark)

5)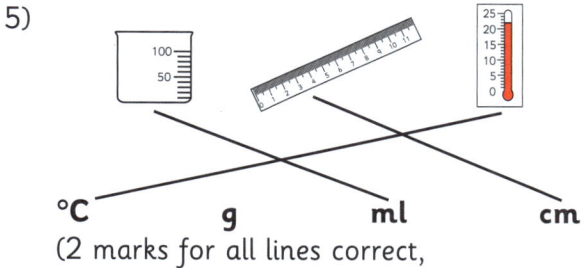
   (2 marks for all lines correct,
   otherwise 1 mark for two lines correct)

6) E.g.

   6 (1 mark)

7) **47 g** (1 mark)

8) You would follow the red path.
   So you end up at letter **B**.
   (1 mark)
   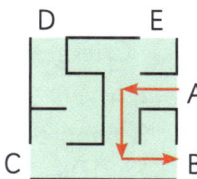

9) This is a **pyramid**.
   Four of its faces are triangles and the
   other face is a **square**.
   It has **8** edges and **5** vertices.
   (2 marks for all four correct, otherwise
   1 mark for at least two correct)

10) 39 − 24 = **15** (1 mark)

11) Count right in 3s until you reach 15, e.g.
    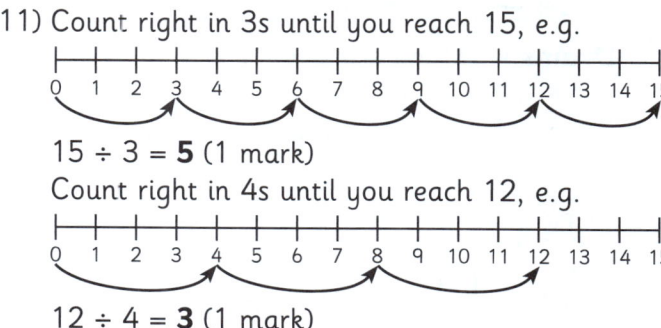
    15 ÷ 3 = **5** (1 mark)
    Count right in 4s until you reach 12, e.g.

    12 ÷ 4 = **3** (1 mark)

12) 20p + 5p = 25p, £1 = 100p
    100p − 25p = **75p** (1 mark)

    Any set of coins that adds to exactly 25p,
    e.g. **10p**, **10p** and **5p** (1 mark)

Section Seven — Statistics

Page 52 — Tables

1) **2** people said their favourite animal was a cat.
   1 person said it was a rabbit.

2) E.g.

Fruit	How many?
Apple	7
Banana	2
Pear	4

3) There were **16** black cars.
   There were 21 − 11 = **10** more
   white cars than blue cars.

Page 53 — Tally Charts

Warm Up: There are two groups
of 5 lines and one set of 3 lines,
so the tally represents 5 + 5 + 3 = **13** eggs.

1)

Flower	Tally	Total
Rose	𝍷𝍷𝍷	15
Buttercup	𝍷𝍷 ⅠⅠ	**12**
Daffodil	𝍷𝍷𝍷 ⅠⅠ	**17**
Daisy	𝍷 ⅠⅠⅠ	8

She saw the most **daffodils**.

Answers

2)

Colour	Tally	Total
Red	|||| |||	8
Yellow	||||		6
Blue	||||	4

Page 54 — Block Diagrams

1) **Drums** was the most popular option.
   5 − 3 = **2** more people said drums than piano.
   4 + 3 + 3 + 5 = **15** pupils were asked in total.

2)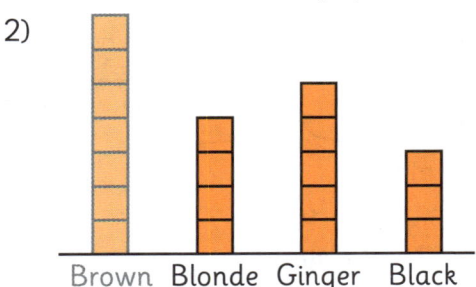

Page 55 — Pictograms

1)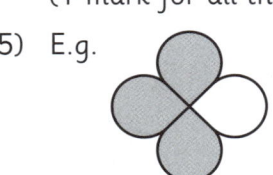

2) Class **2C** got the most points.
   Class 2A got 9 − 7 = **2** fewer points than class 2B.

3)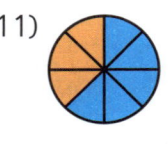

Pages 56-59 — Year Two Objectives Test

1)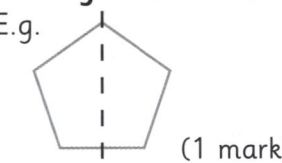
   (1 mark — accept 64 or 66)

2) **6 + 6 + 6 = 18** (or **3 + 3 + 3 + 3 + 3 + 3 = 18**)
   (1 mark)

3) **Pentagon** (1 mark)
   E.g.
   (1 mark)

4) 10, 8, 12, 30 and 20 are even.
   10, 15, 45, 30 and 20 are in the five times table.

   (1 mark for all three circled)

5) E.g.
   3 of the sections should be shaded. (1 mark)

6) 38 > **37**
   41 < **43**
   30 + 9 = **39**
   (2 marks for all correct, otherwise 1 mark for at least one correct)

7)
   (1 mark for both boxes ticked)

8) Split 9 into 3 equal groups.
   She gives away 9 ÷ 3 = **3** toy pigs. (1 mark)

9) He has 50p + 20p + 20p = 90p.
   So he has 90p − 60p = **30p** left. (1 mark)

10) E.g. Using partitioning:
    34 = 30 + 4, 23 = 20 + 3
    Subtract the tens: 30 − 20 = 10
    Subtract the ones: 4 − 3 = 1
    10 + 1 = 11, so he has **11** more planes.
    (1 mark)

11) (1 mark)

12) Football
    Rugby
    Cricket (1 mark)
    4 + 4 + 2 = 10 people chose football.
    3 people chose rugby.
    So 10 − 3 = **7** more people chose football.
    (1 mark)